Smart Phonics 2

e-future

Smart PhOnics 2 Contents

Smart Phonics

Phonics for Reading and Writing

PhOnics

Awareness of Letter-Sound Relationships	Skills to Blend Sounds to Make Meaningful Words
a - /a/ as in apple 	• Vowel + Consonant a + t → at
b - /b/ as in book 	• Consonant + Vowel + Consonant
c - /k/ as in cat 	b + at → bat c + at → cat
t - /t/ as in tiger 	h + at → hat

! Children with phonics skills are able to read and write many English words without relying on memorization or guessing.

Sounds Introduced in the Smart Phonics Series

Book 1	**Single Letters**	a, b, c, d, e, f, g, h, i, j, k, l, m, n, o, p, q, r, s, t, u, v, w, x, y, z	
Book 2	**Short Vowels**	a, e, i, o, u	
Book 3	**Long Vowels**	a_e, i _e, o_e, u_e	
Book 4	**Two Letter Consonants**	Consonant Blends	bl, cl, fl, gl, pl, sl, br, cr, dr, fr, pr, sm, sn, st, sw, nk
		Consonant Digraphs	ch, sh, th, wh, ng
Book 5	**Two Letter Vowels**	Vowel Digraphs	ee, ea, ai, ay, oa, ow (bowl), oo (book), oo (moon)
		Vowel Diphthongs	oi, oy, ou, ow (clown)
		R-controlled Vowels	ar, er, ir, or, ur

Goals of Smart Phonics 2

- Children learn to make two letter combinations of short vowels and consonants.
- Children learn to make three letter combinations of short vowels and consonants.
- Children learn words with the "consonant - short vowel - consonant" combination.
- Children learn sight words through the phonics stories.

1. Short Vowel + Consonant

a + t → a t

e + t → e t

i + t → i t

o + t → o t

u + t → u t

2. Consonant + Vowel + Consonant

c + a t → c a t

n + e t → n e t

s + i t → s i t

p + o t → p o t

c + u t → c u t

Note to Teachers

The ultimate goal for the Smart Phonics series is to guide children to develop phonics skills, namely to identify the English sounds and letters and understand the relationships between them. We advise teachers to focus on the enhancement of phonics skills throughout the course rather than emphasizing the spelling of words.

Lesson Flow

Introduction

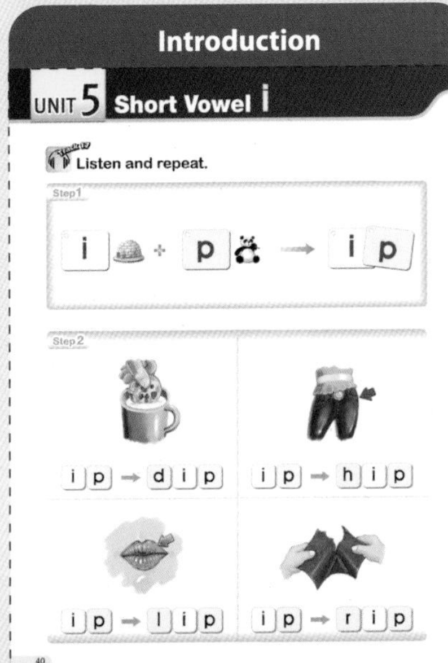

New target combinations of sounds and related words are introduced.

Reading (words)

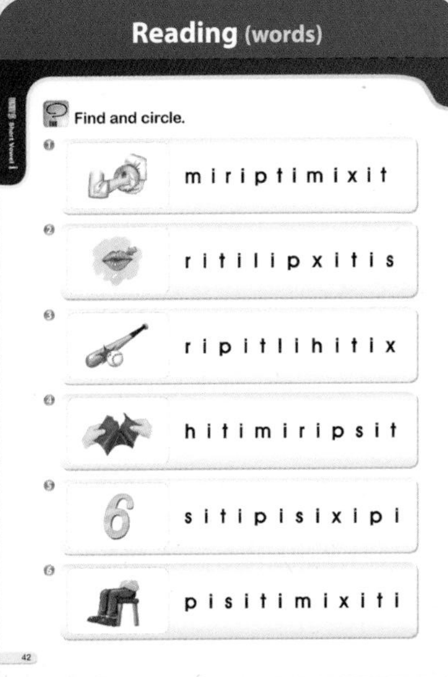

Children practice reading words with the target sounds.

Listening

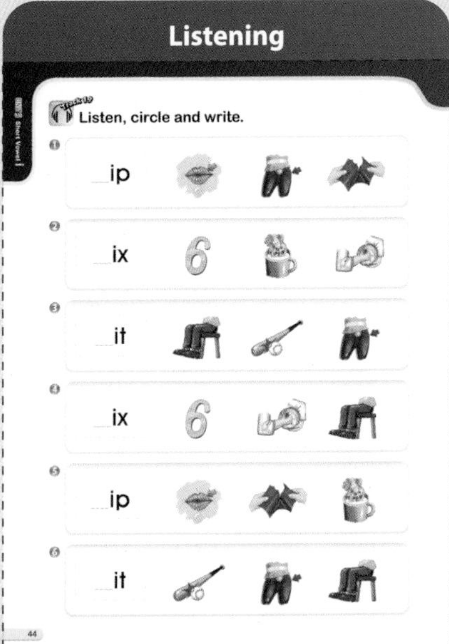

Children consolidate the target words through a listening activity.

Reading (sentences)

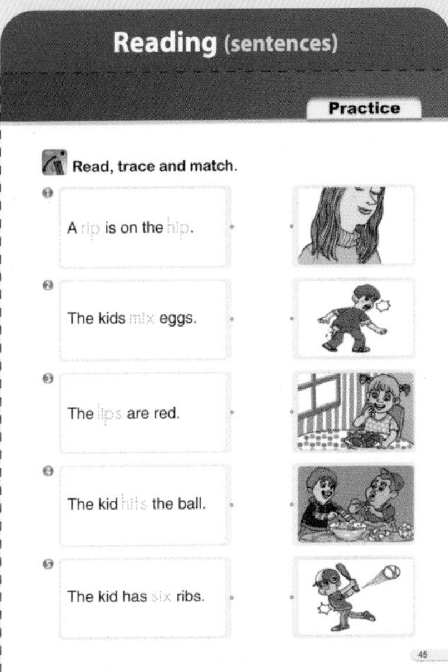

Children practice reading sentences with the target words.

Story

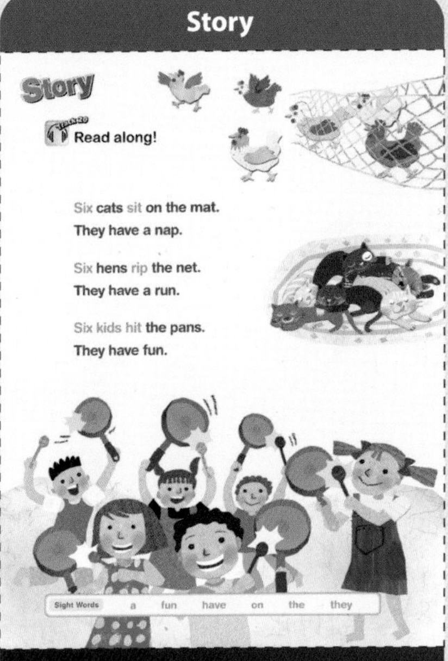

Children will further practice reading the words they learned through a fun phonics story. They will be naturally exposed to sight words as well.

Writing

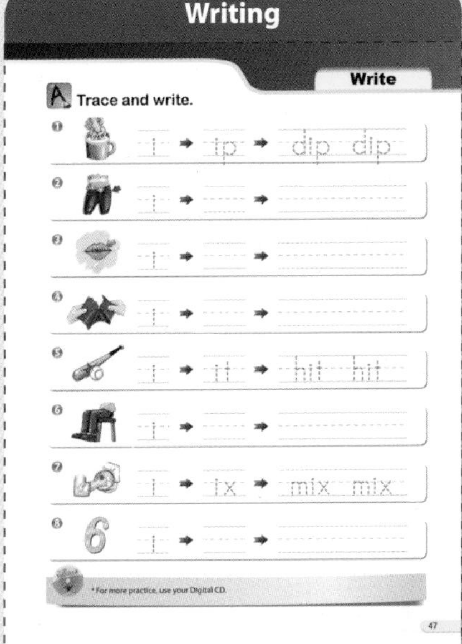

The target sounds and words are consolidated through a writing activity.

Fun Elements

Comics

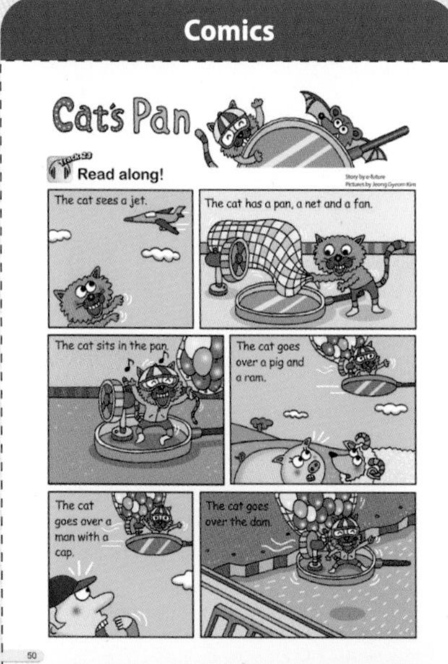

Children will review the words they learned through entertaining comics. They will be naturally exposed to sight words as well.

Board Games

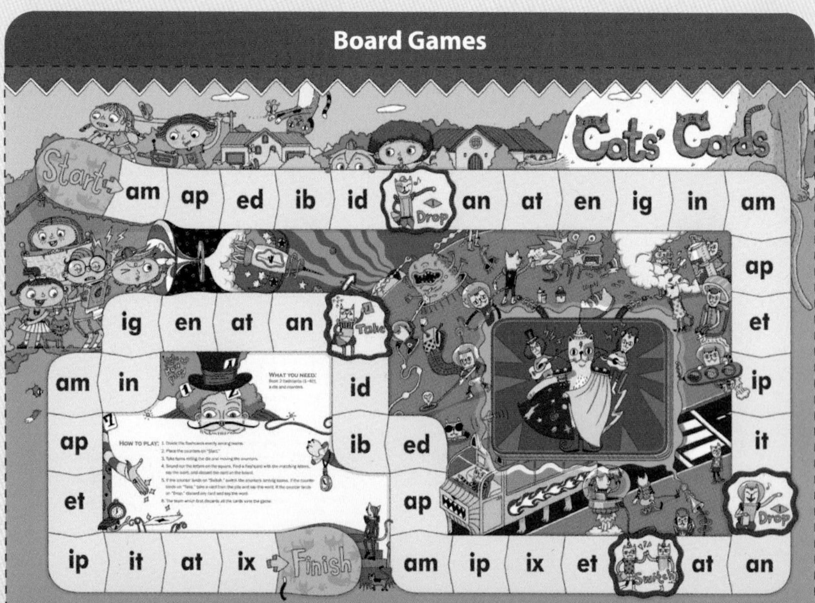

Three interesting board games for phonics are provided in the book. The game boards are creatively illustrated to grab children's attention. The intention is to have fun while practicing phonics skills.

Smart Phonics App

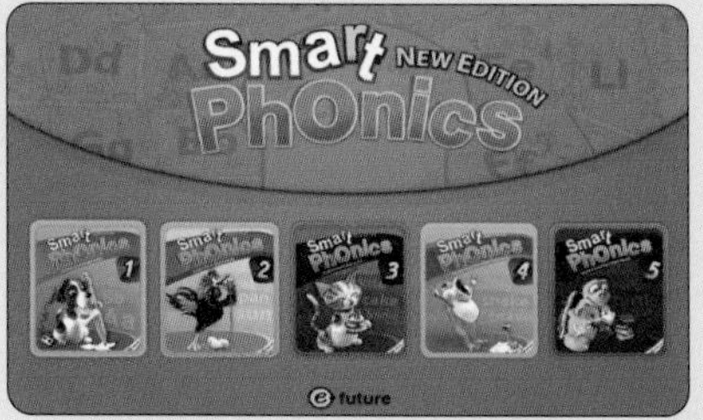

Free App

- ▶ Audio
- ▶ Digital Contents
  Flashcards, practice activities, games, stories

Smart Phonics Online

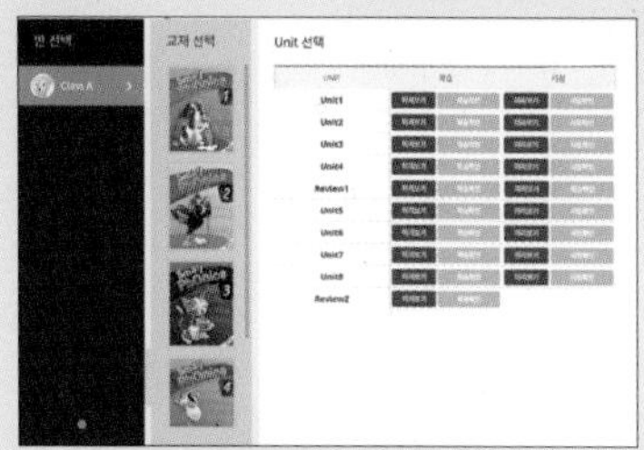

www.eSmartClass.net

- ▶ LCMS (Learning Content Management System)
- ▶ Interactive e-book and additional practice
- ▶ Downloadable resources

UNIT 1 Short Vowel a

Track 1

Listen and repeat.

Step 1

Step 2

a m → d a m

a m → h a m

a m → j a m

a m → r a m

Listen and repeat.

Step 1

Step 2

a p → c a p

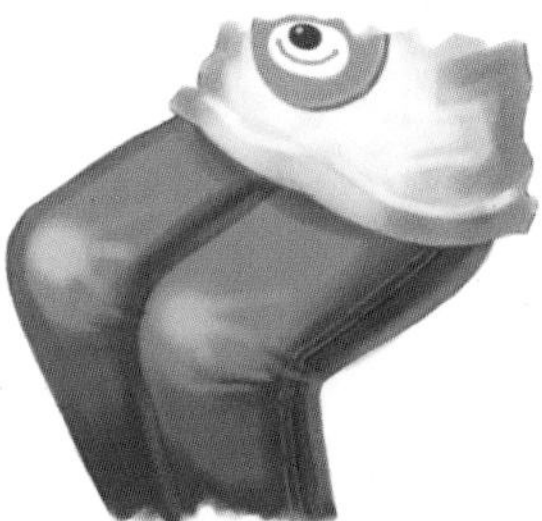

a p → l a p

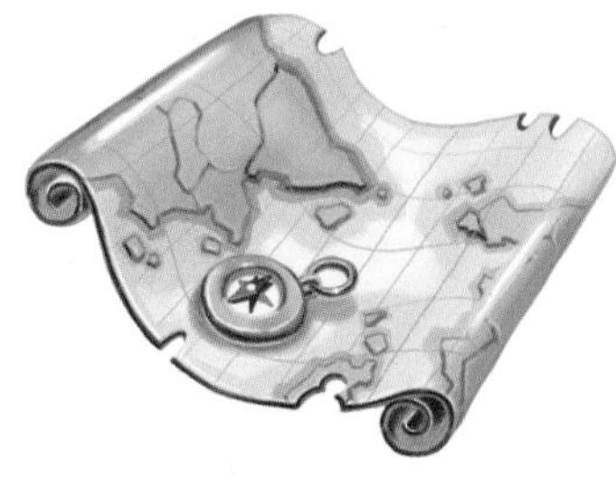

a p → m a p

a p → n a p

Read and color.

1. ham

2. cap

3. lap

4. ram

5. map

6. dam

Circle and write.

1. am / ap

j a m

2. 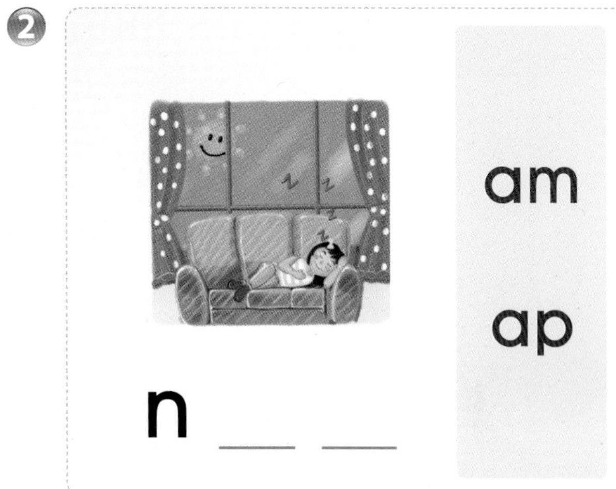

am / ap

n __ __

3. 

am / ap

d __ __

4. 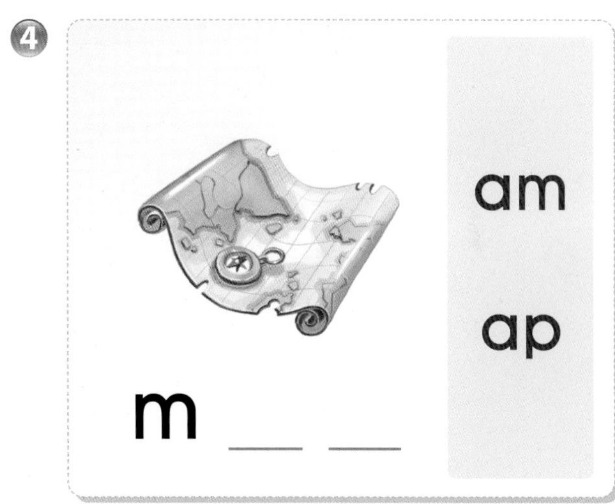

am / ap

m __ __

5. 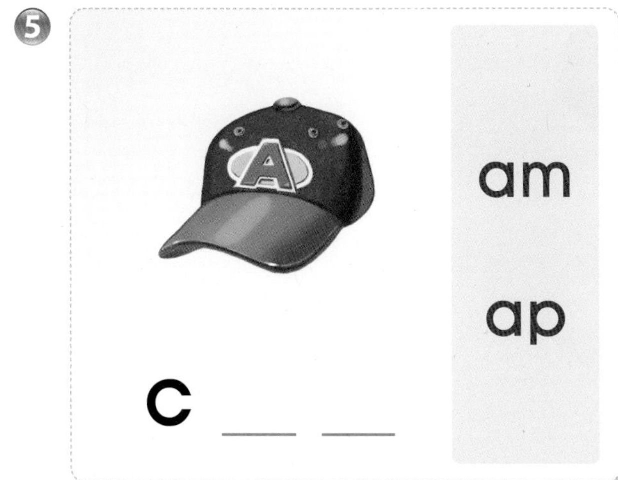

am / ap

c __ __

6. 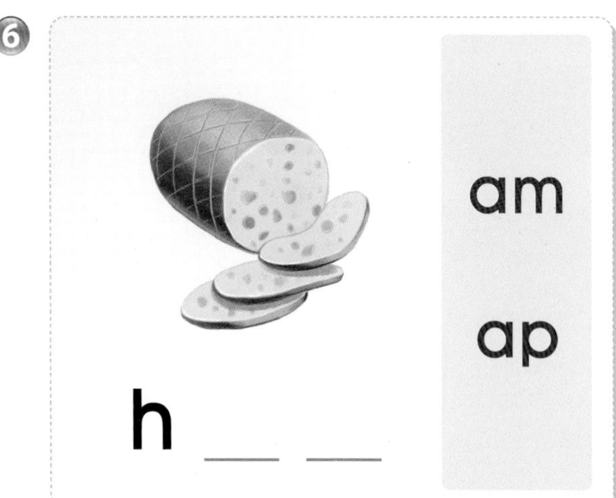

am / ap

h __ __

Track 3 Listen and circle.

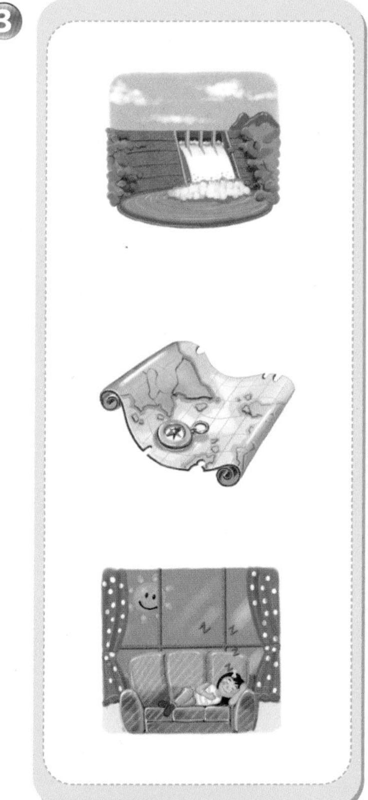

Read and check.

- ○ The ram has jam.
- ○ The ram has ham.

- ○ The ram has a nap.
- ○ The ram has a map.

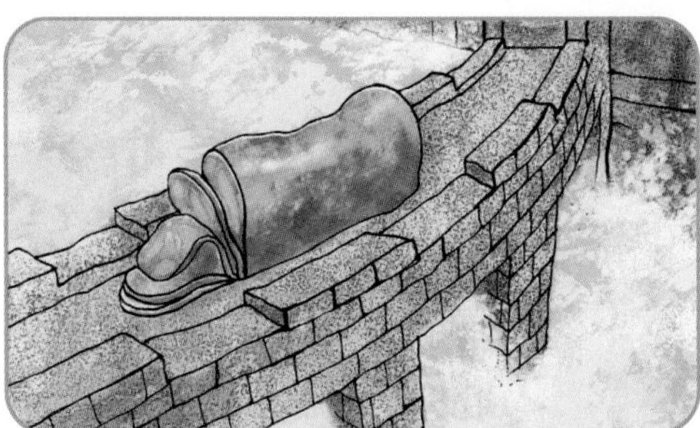

- ○ The ram is on the dam.
- ○ The ham is on the dam.

- ○ The jam is on the map.
- ○ The jam is on the lap.

- ○ A cap is on the dam.
- ○ A cap is on the lap.

Story

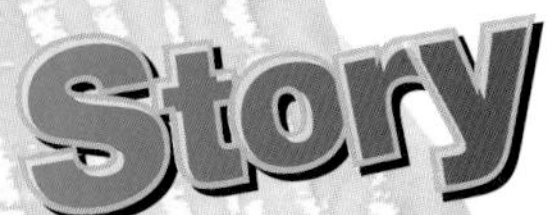

Track 4

Read along!

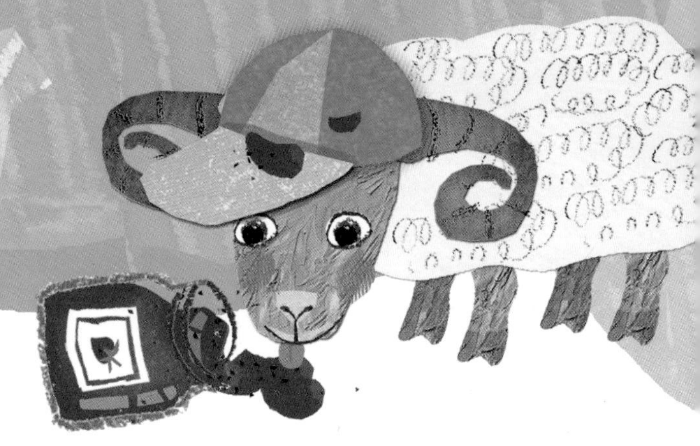

The ram has a cap.
The ram has jam.
Oh! The ram has jam on his cap.

The ram has a map.
The ram has a nap.
Oh! The ram has a nap on his map.

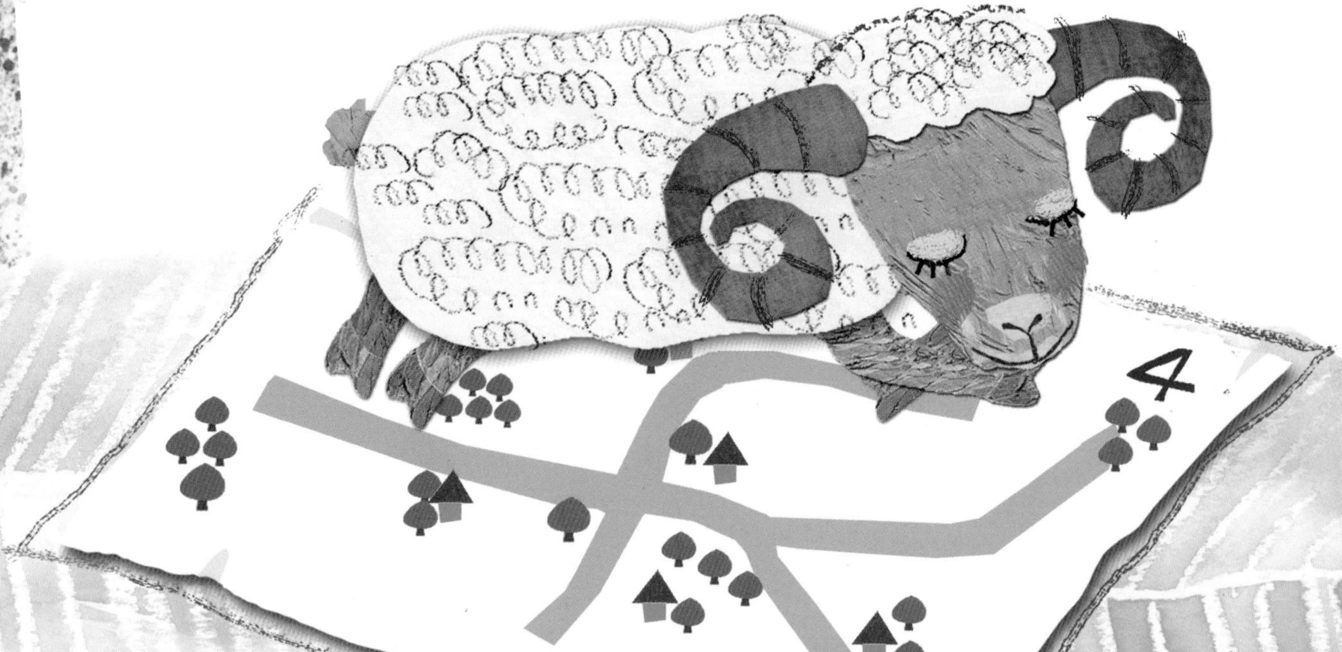

Sight Words	a	has	his	oh	on	the

Trace and write.

1 a → am → dam dam

2 a → →

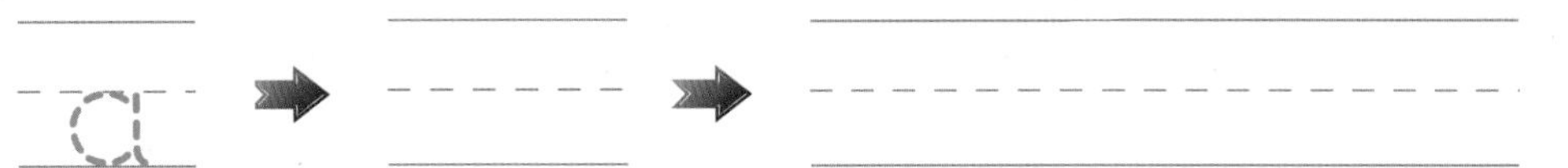

3 a → →

4 a → →

5 a → ap → cap cap

6 a → →

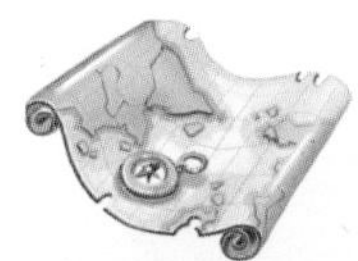

7 a → →

8 a → →

UNIT 2 Short Vowel a

Track 5

Listen and repeat.

Step 1

Step 2

a n → c a n

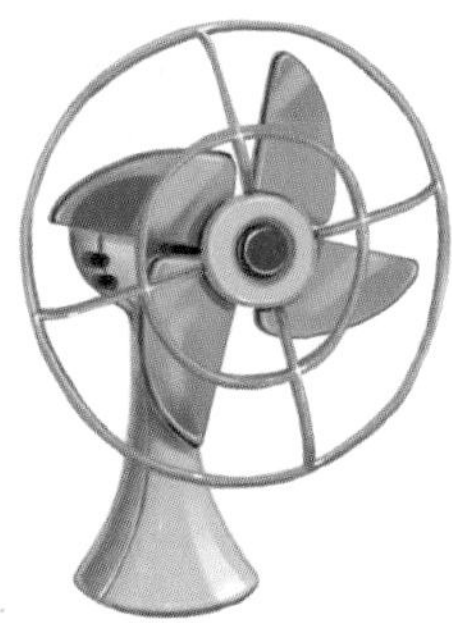

a n → f a n

a n → m a n

a n → p a n

Listen and repeat.

Step 1

Step 2

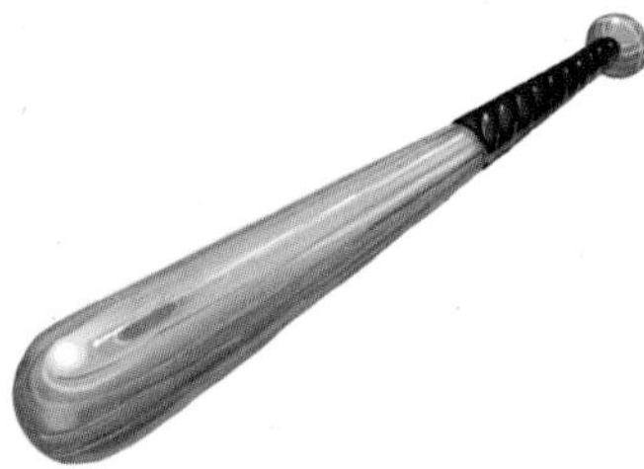

a t → b a t

a t → c a t

a t → h a t

a t → m a t

Read and color.

1 can

2 mat

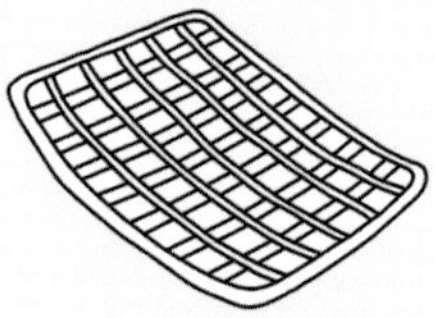

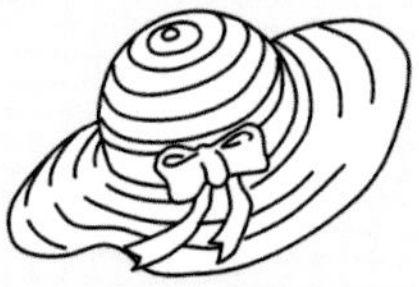

3 hat

4 pan

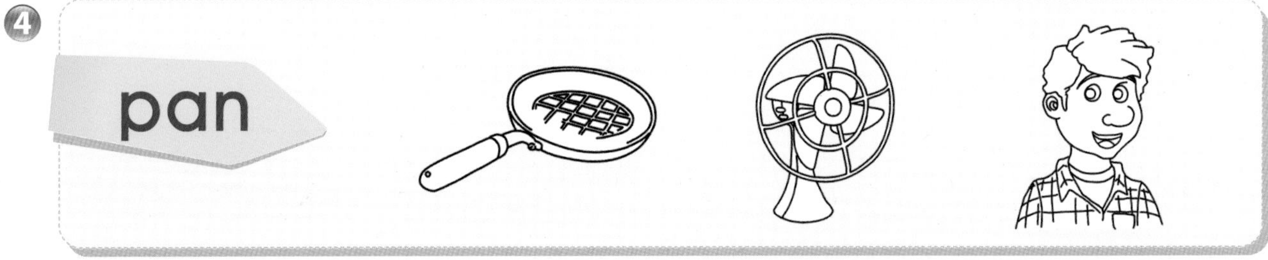

5 man

6 cat

Circle and write.

1

an

at

b ___ ___

2

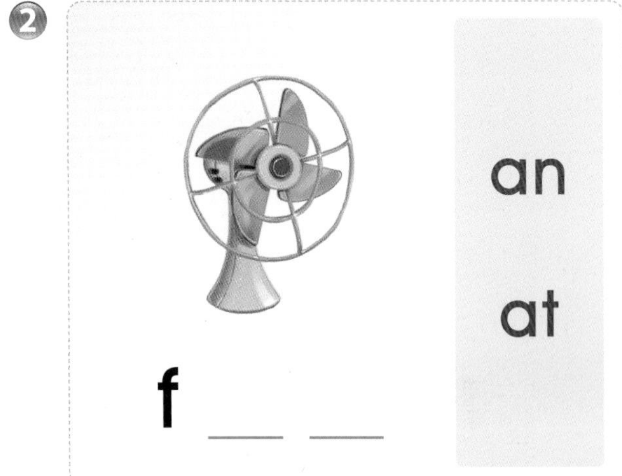

an

at

f ___ ___

3

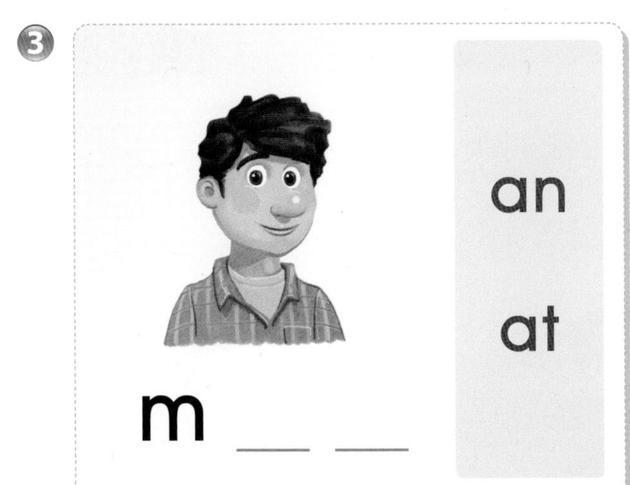

an

at

m ___ ___

4

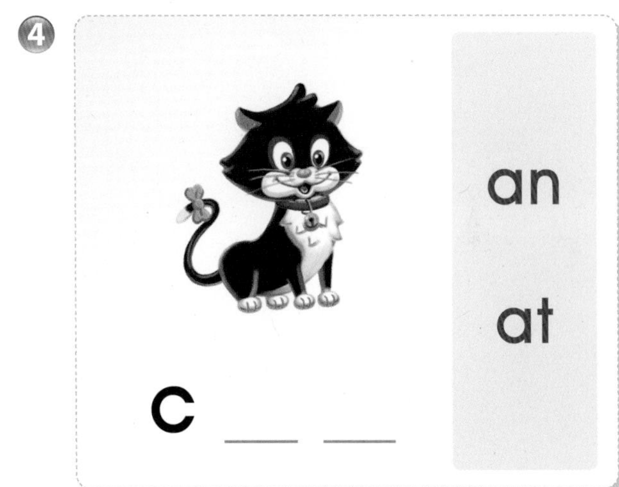

an

at

c ___ ___

5

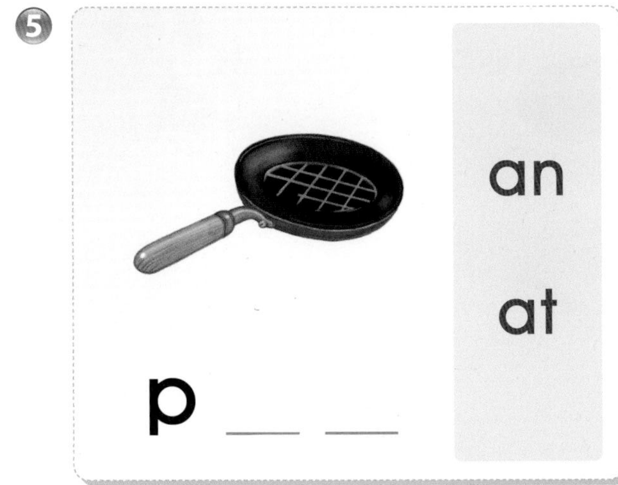

an

at

p ___ ___

6

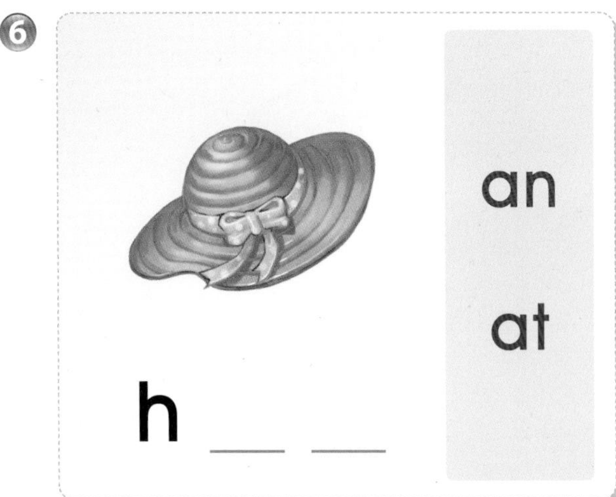

an

at

h ___ ___

Track 7

Listen and circle.

1
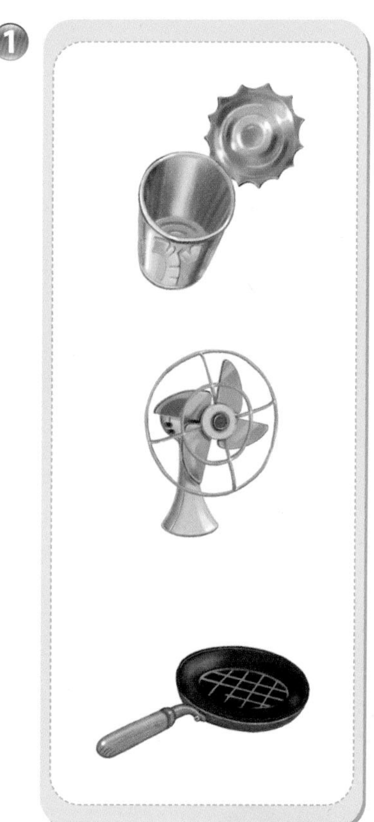

2
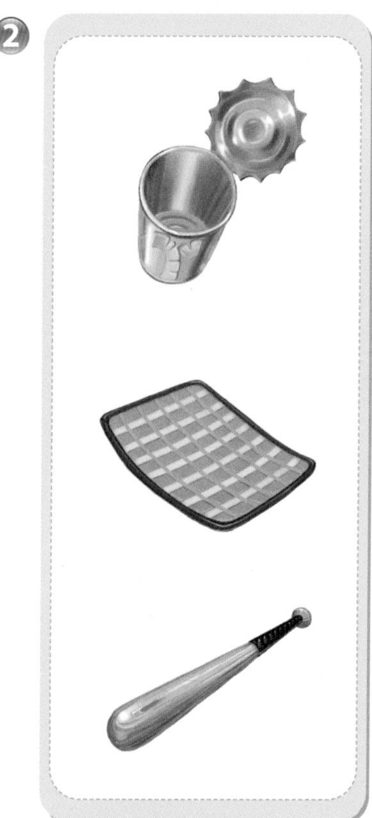

3

4

5

6

Read and check.

1

- ◯ A bat is in the fan.
- ◯ A bat is in the can.

2

- ◯ The pan is on the mat.
- ◯ The fan is on the mat.

3

- ◯ The man is on the mat.
- ◯ The man is on the hat.

4

- ◯ The man has a bat.
- ◯ The man has a hat.

5

- ◯ The cat is on the fan.
- ◯ The cat is on the man.

Story

Track 8 Read along!

The cat is on the mat.
The cat has a can.

The cat is on the mat.
The cat has a hat.

The cat is on the mat.
The cat has a fan.

Oh! Goodbye, hat!

Sight Words a goodbye has is oh on the

Trace and write.

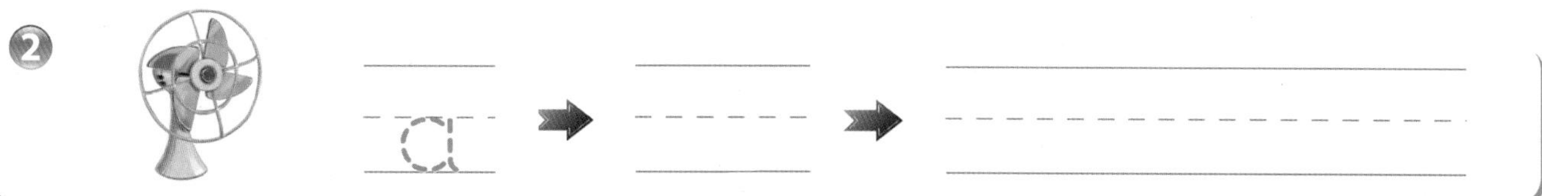

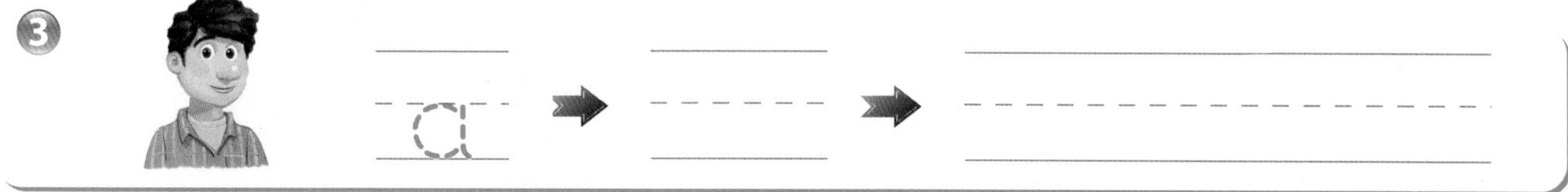

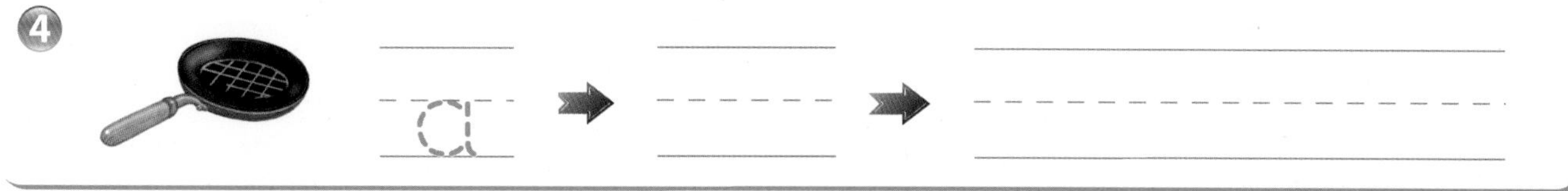

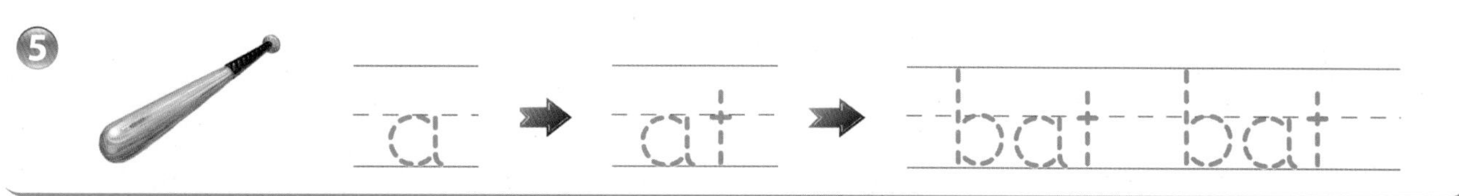

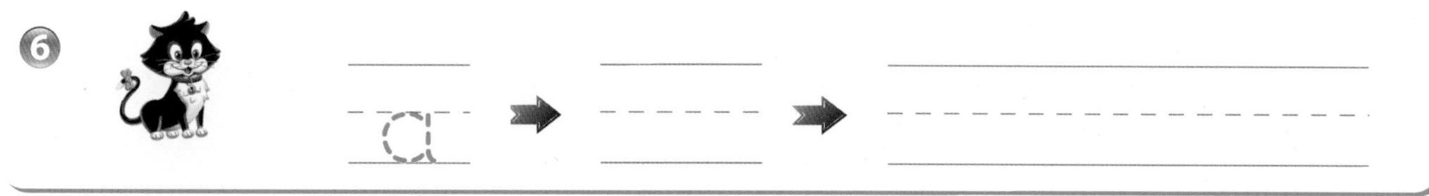

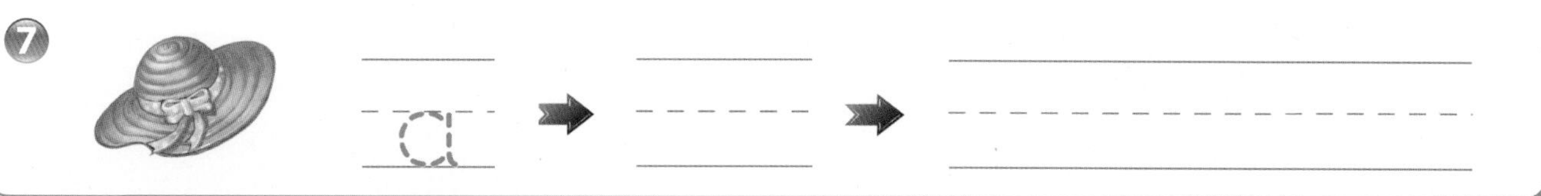

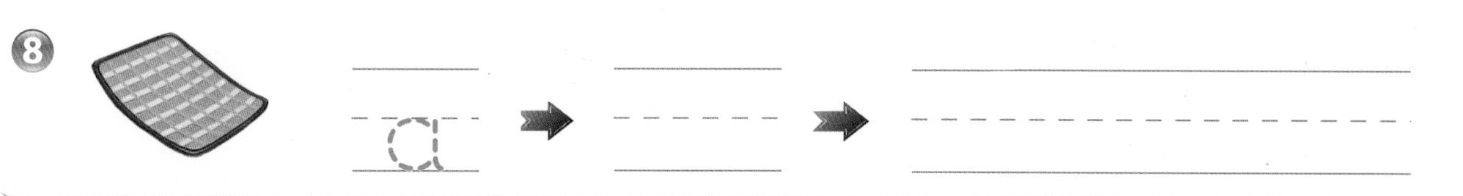

UNIT 3 Short Vowel e

Track 9

Listen and repeat.

Step 1

Step 2

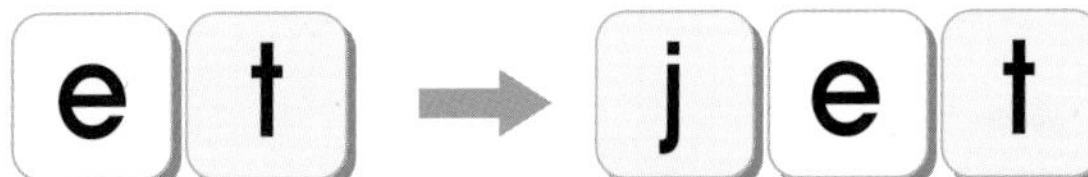

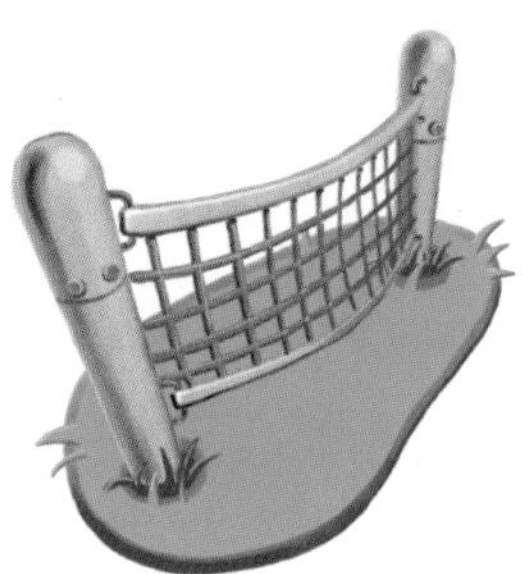

e t → n e t

e t → v e t

e t → w e t

Listen and repeat.

Step 2

ed → bed

ed → red

en → hen

en → pen

Read and color.

1. bed

2. wet

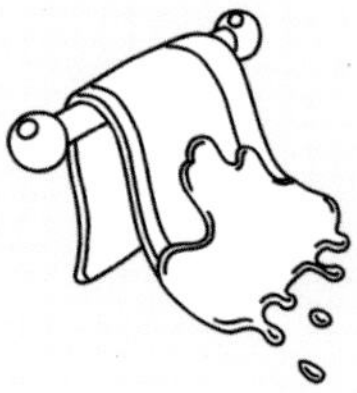

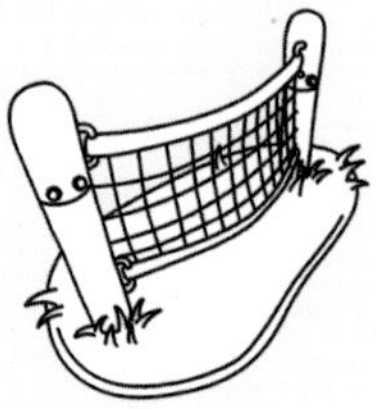

3. hen

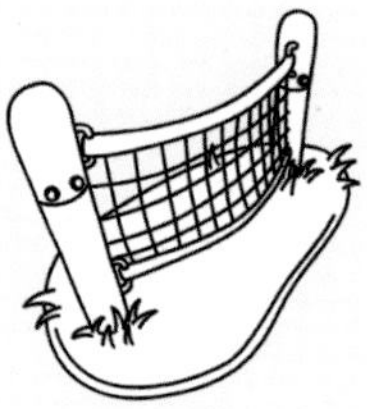

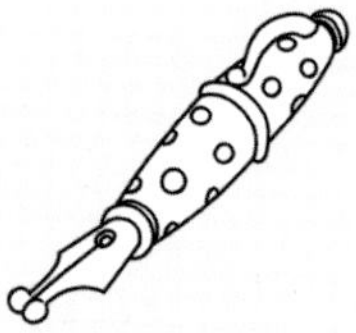

4. vet

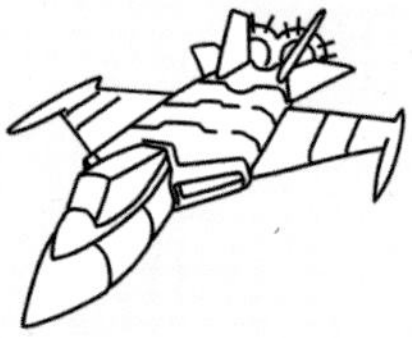

5. jet

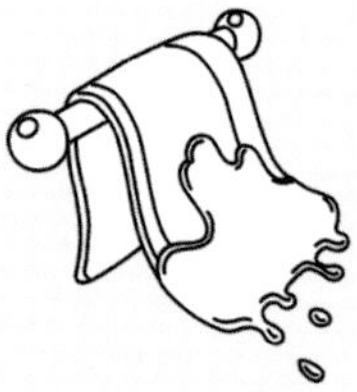

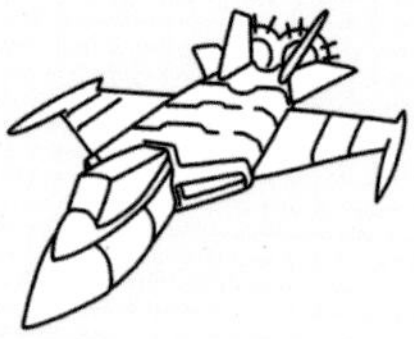

6. pen

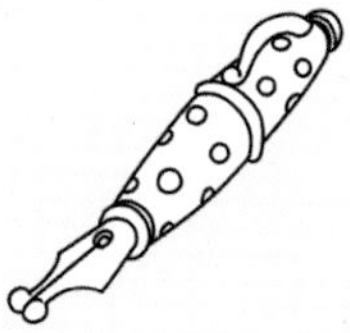

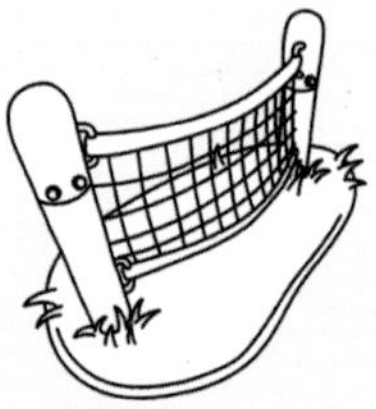

Circle and write.

1

et
ed
en

r __ __

2

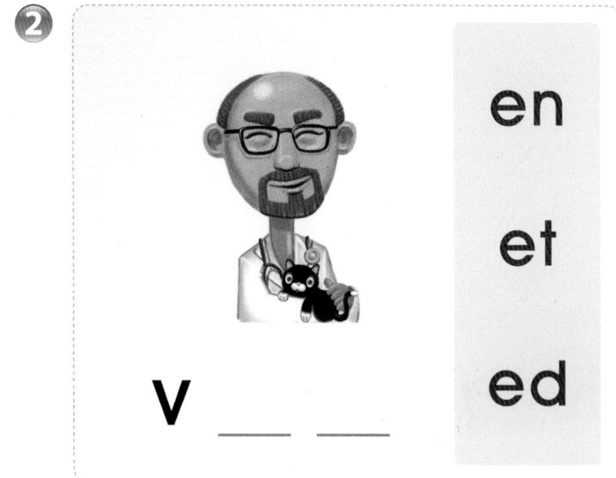

en
et
ed

v __ __

3

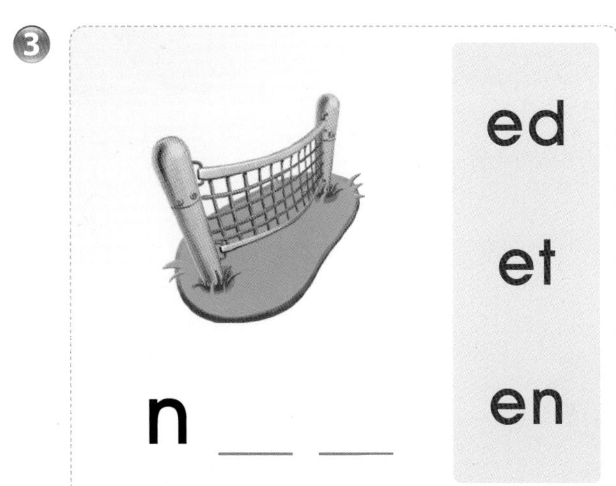

ed
et
en

n __ __

4

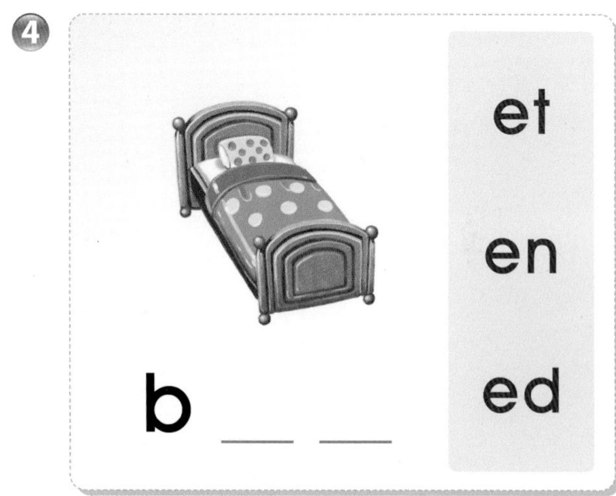

et
en
ed

b __ __

5

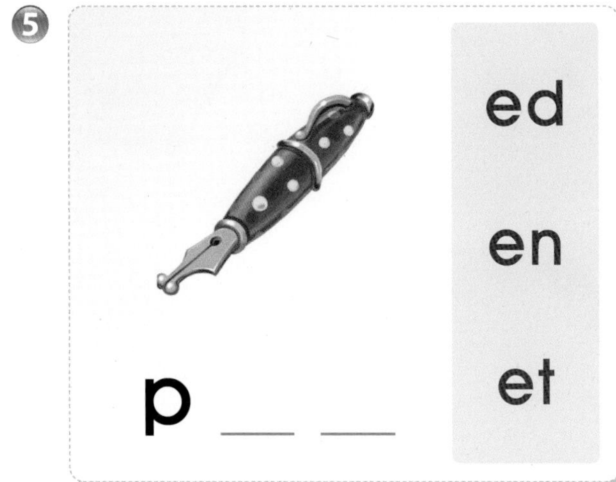

ed
en
et

p __ __

6

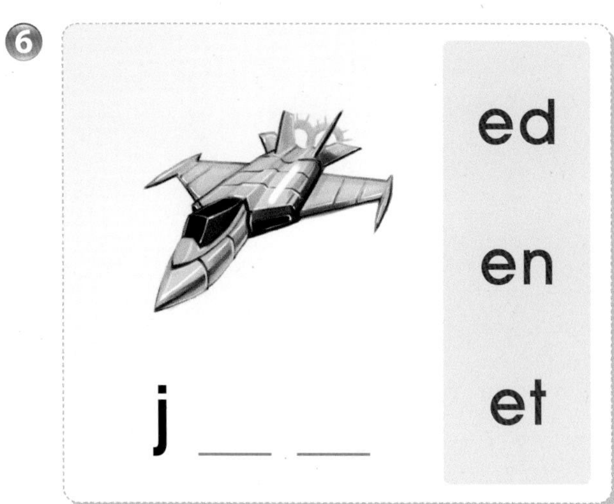

ed
en
et

j __ __

Track 11

Listen and circle.

1

2

3
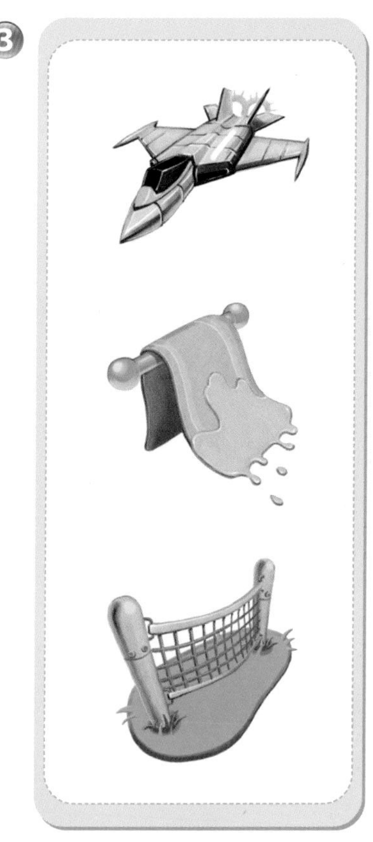

4

5
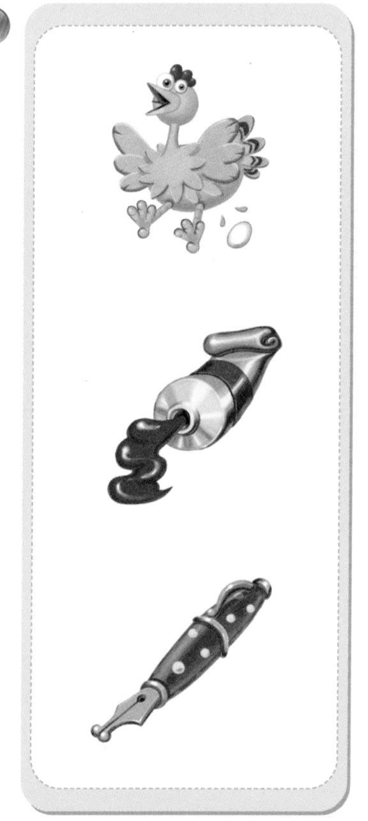

6

Read and check.

1

- ◯ The bed is wet.
- ◯ The bed is red.

2
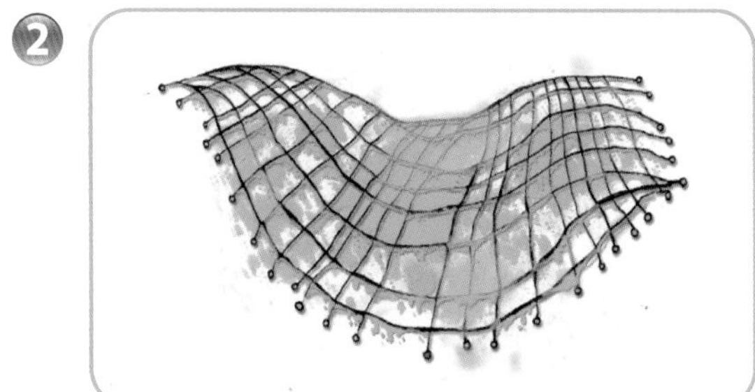

- ◯ The net is wet.
- ◯ The jet is wet.

3

- ◯ The hen is on the jet.
- ◯ The hen is on the vet.

4
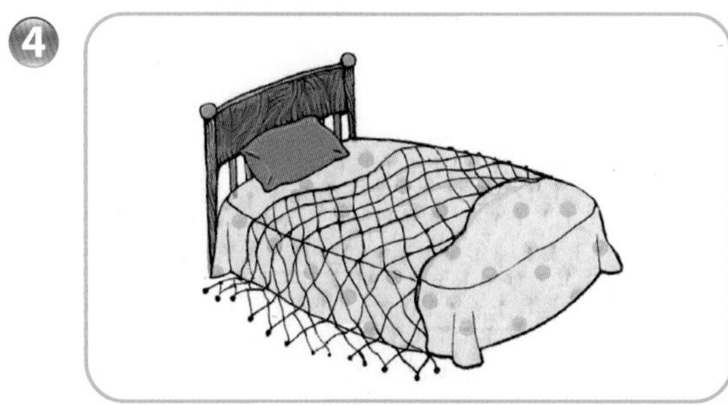

- ◯ The net is on the jet.
- ◯ The net is on the bed.

5

- ◯ The vet has a hen.
- ◯ The vet has a pen.

Story

Track 12

Read along!

The man goes to the **bed**.
The **bed** is **red**.

The **hen** goes to the **bed**.
The **bed** is **wet**.

The **hen** has a nap.
Oh! The **hen** is **red**!

Sight Words	goes	has	is	oh	the	to

Trace and write.

1. e → et → jet jet
2. e → →
3. e → →
4. e → →
5. e → ed → bed bed
6. e → →
7. e → en → hen hen
8. e → →

UNIT 4 Short Vowel i

Track 13

Listen and repeat.

Step 1

Step 2

i b → b i b

i b → r i b

i d → k i d

i d → l i d

Listen and repeat.

Step 1

Step 2

i g → p i g

i g → w i g

i n → f i n

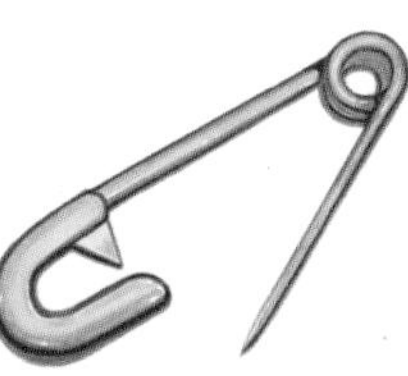

i n → p i n

Find and circle.

p o l i e a f i n i p i

n a l i d o g i f i d i

3

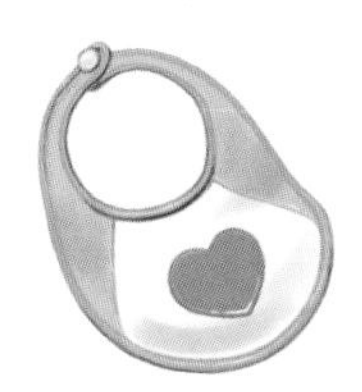

l i b i b o i p i e n i

4

p i p g i o i w i g d

5

p i d a p i n d u p i f

6

d k a p o p i g i g o d

 Choose and write.

bib fin wig rib pig kid

1

2

3

4

5

6

Track 15

Listen, circle and write.

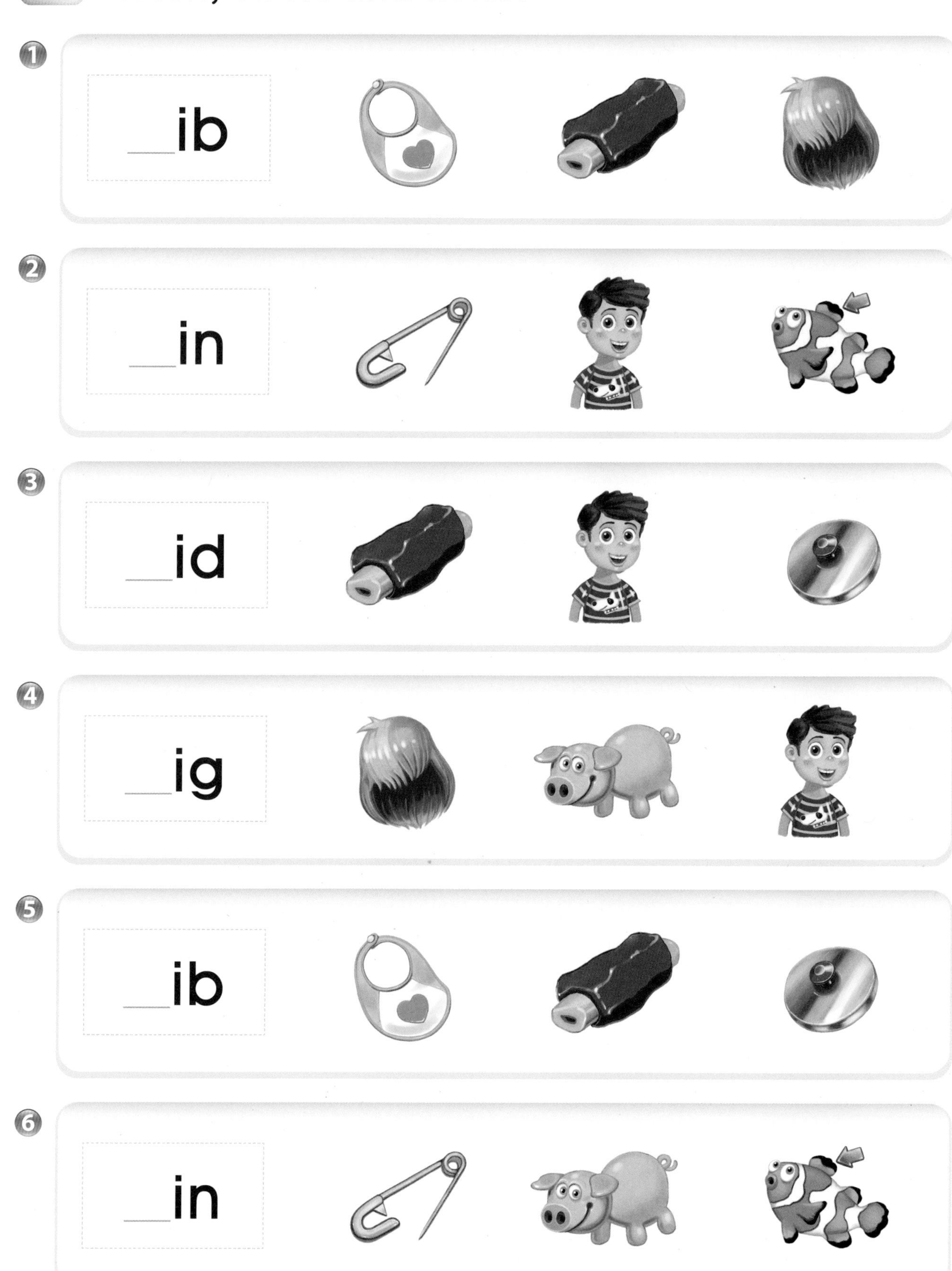

Read, trace and match.

1. The pin is on the lid.

2. The bib is on the wig.

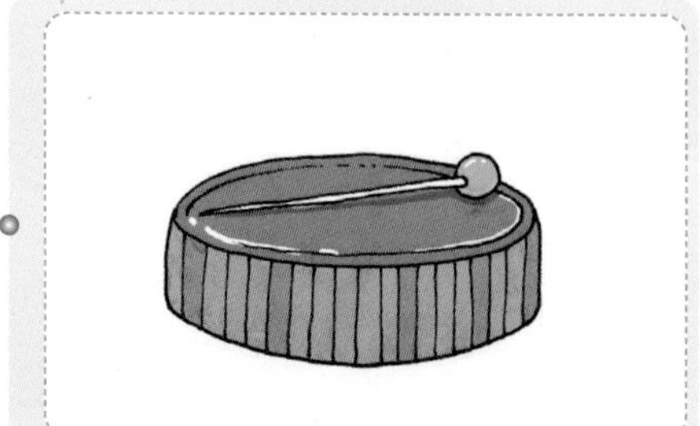

3. The kid has a pin.

4. The kid has a rib.

5. The kid has a pig.

Story

Track 16

Read along!

The kid has a bib.
The kid has a rib.

The ram sees the bib.
The ram sees the rib.

The ram has the rib.
Oh, the kid has a wig!

Sight Words a has oh sees the

Trace and write.

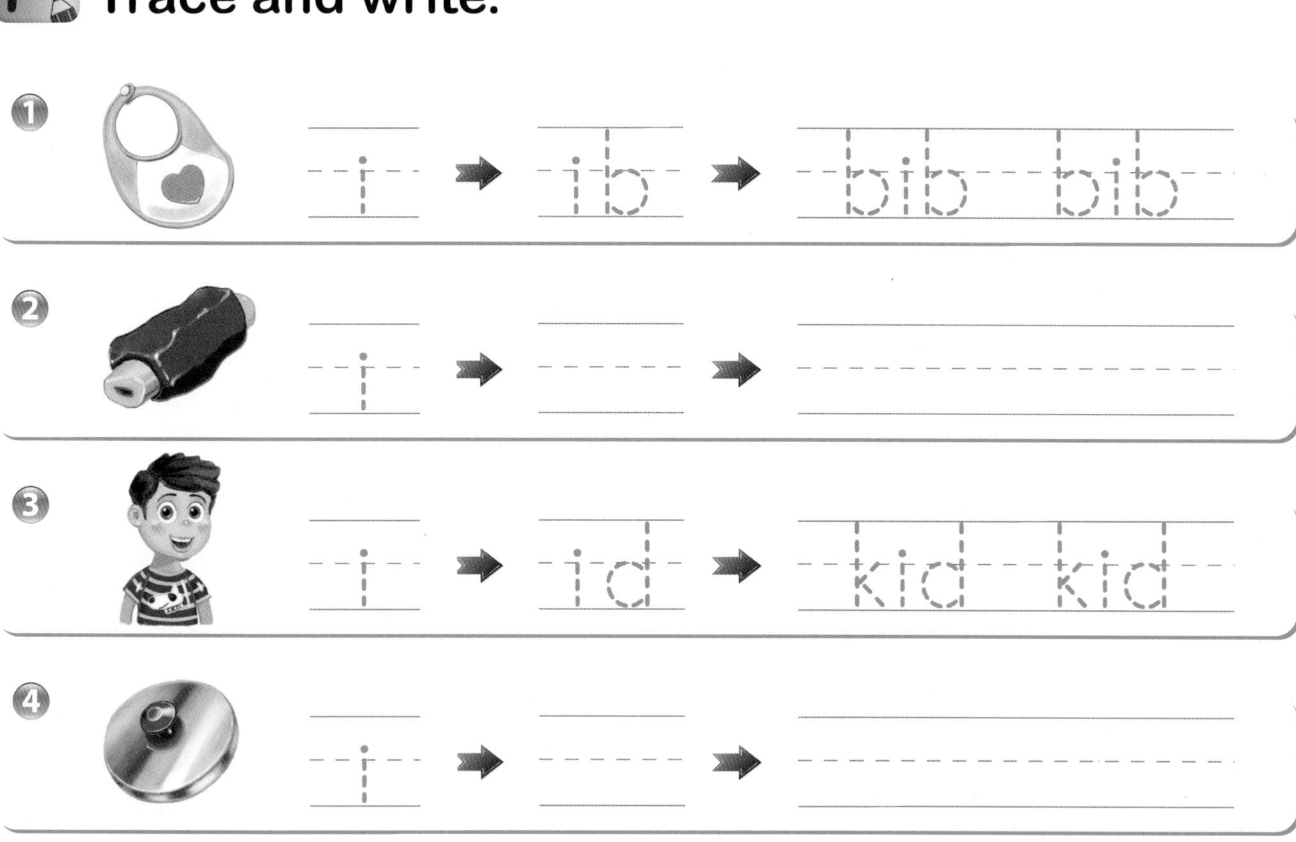

1 i → ib → bib bib

2 i →

3 i → id → kid kid

4 i →

5 i → ig → pig pig

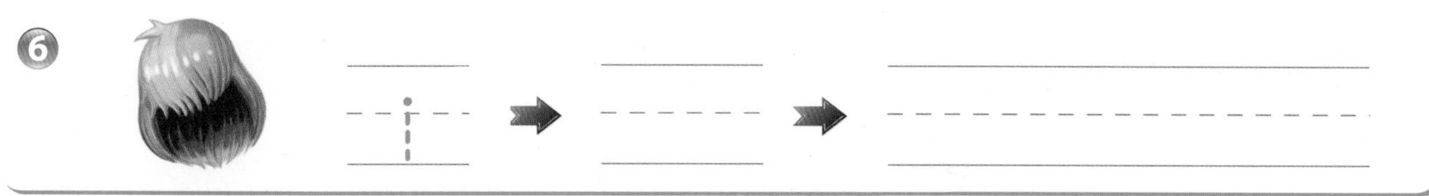

6 i →

7 i → in → fin fin

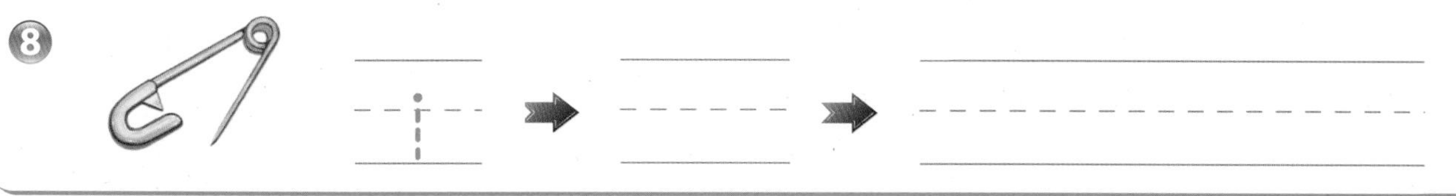

8 i →

UNIT 5 Short Vowel i

Track 17
Listen and repeat.

Step 1

Step 2

i p → d i p

i p → h i p

i p → l i p

i p → r i p

Listen and repeat.

Step 1

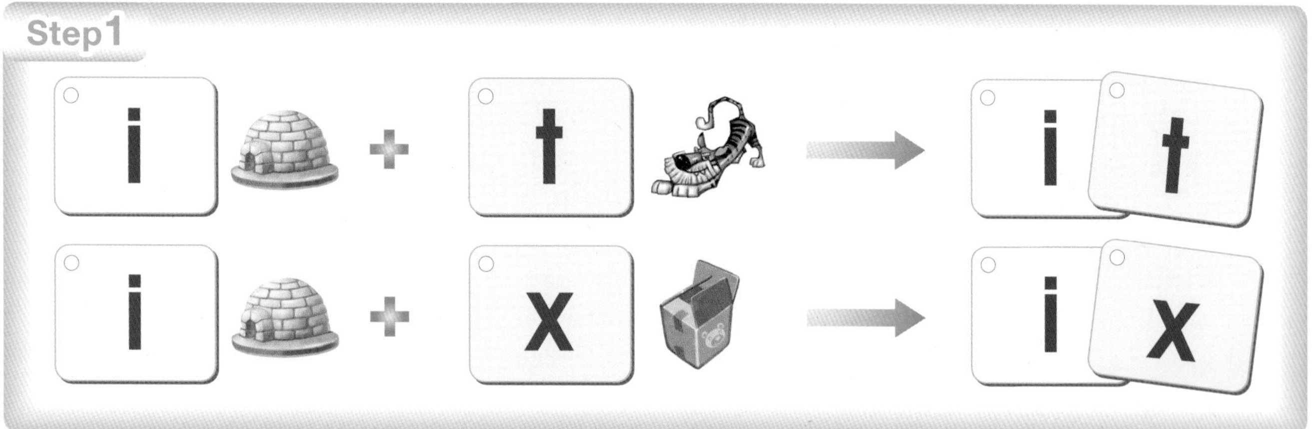

Step 2

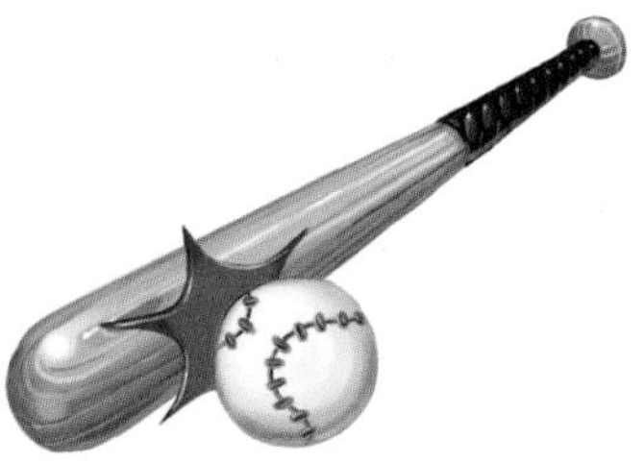

i t → h i t

i t → s i t

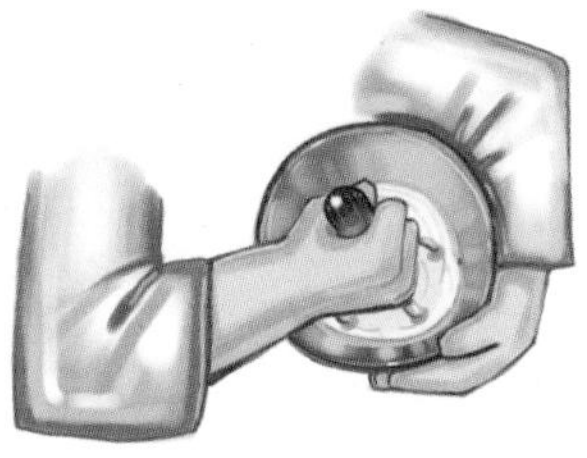

i x → m i x

i x → s i x

Find and circle.

1

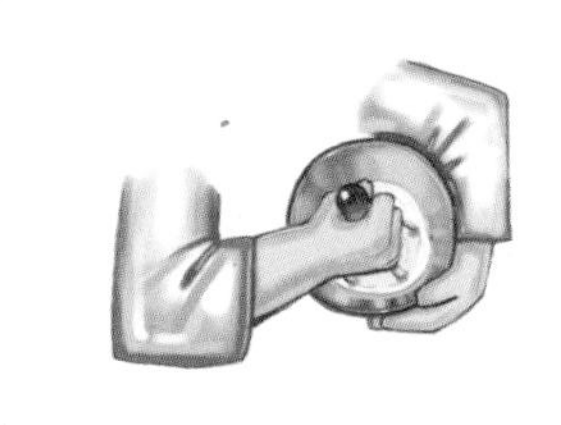

m i r i p t i m i x i t

2

r i t i l i p x i t i s

3

r i p i t l i h i t i x

4

h i t i m i r i p s i t

5

s i t i p i s i x i p i

6

p i s i t i m i x i t i

 Choose and write.

lip hit rip hip six sit

①

②

③

④

⑤

⑥

Track 19

Listen, circle and write.

1. ___ip

2. ___ix

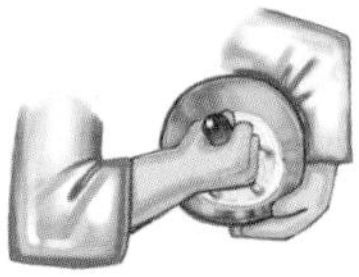

3. ___it

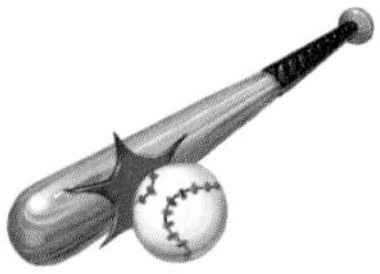

4. ___ix

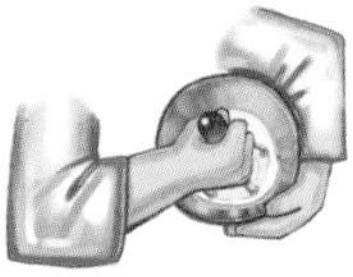

5. ___ip

6. ___it

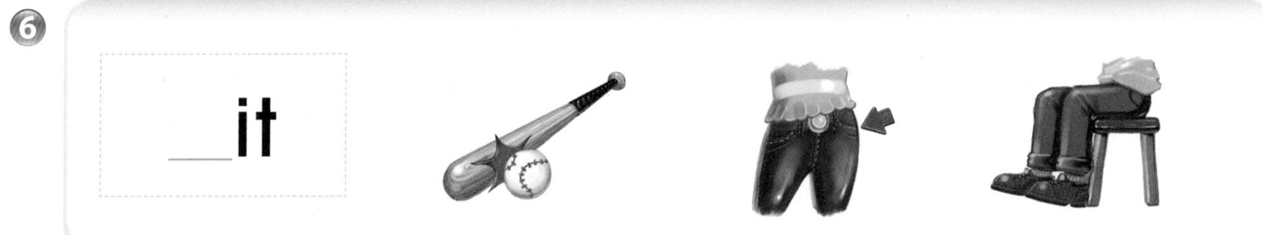

Read, trace and match.

1. A rip is on the hip.
2. The kids mix eggs.
3. The lips are red.
4. The kid hits the ball.
5. The kid has six ribs.

Story

Track 20

Read along!

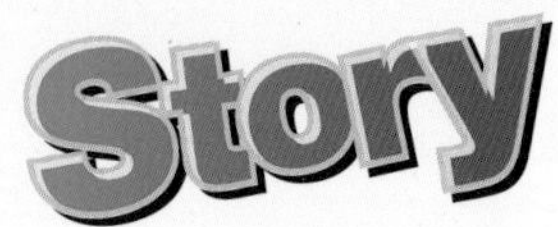

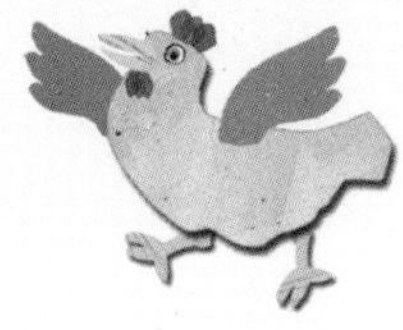

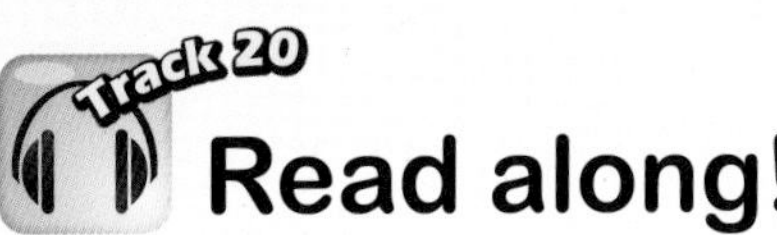

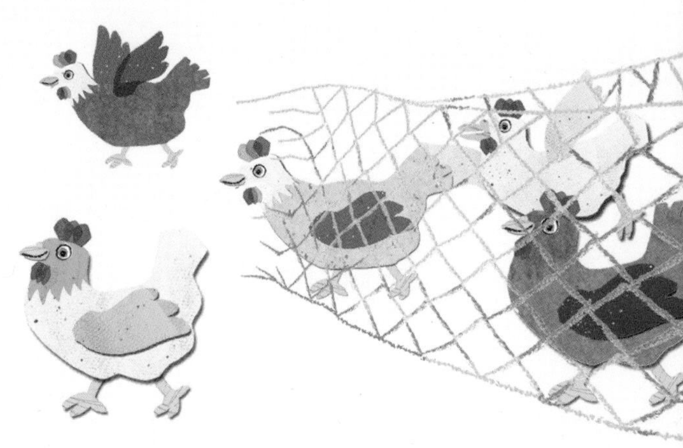

Six cats sit on the mat.

They have a nap.

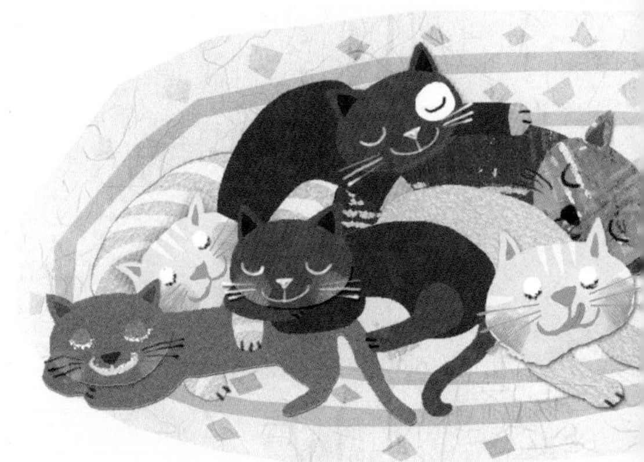

Six hens rip the net.

They have a run.

Six kids hit the pans.

They have fun.

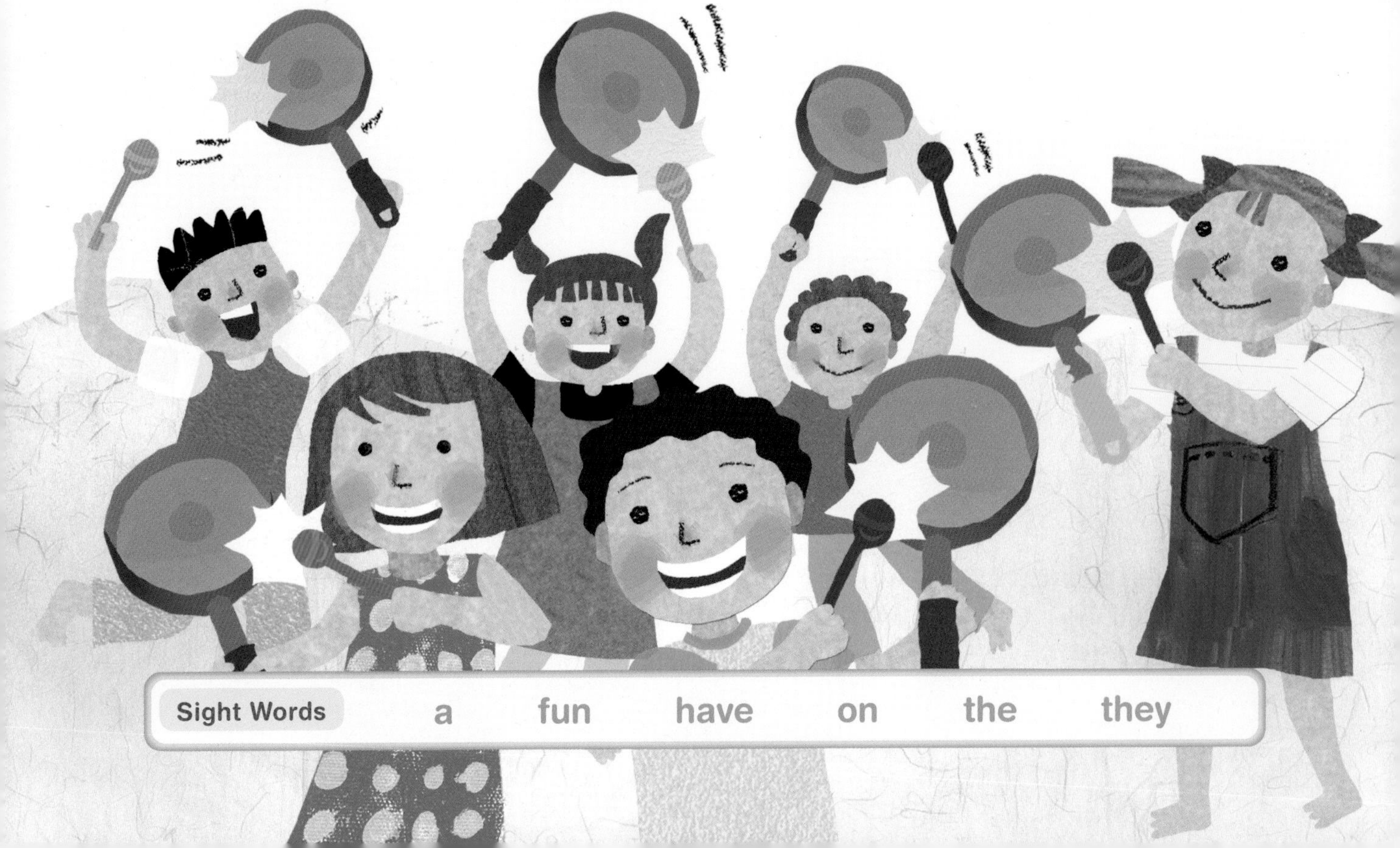

Sight Words	a	fun	have	on	the	they

Trace and write.

1. i → ip → dip dip
2. i → →
3. i → →
4. i → →
5. i → it → hit hit
6. i → →
7. i → ix → mix mix
8. i → →

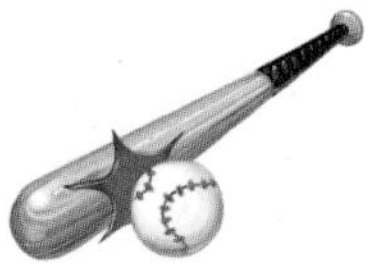

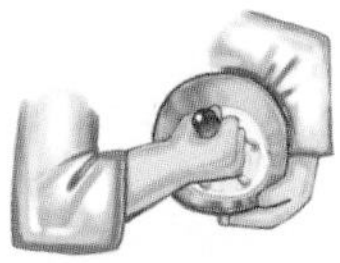

REVIEW 1 Short Vowels a · e · i

Track 21

Listen and color.

1

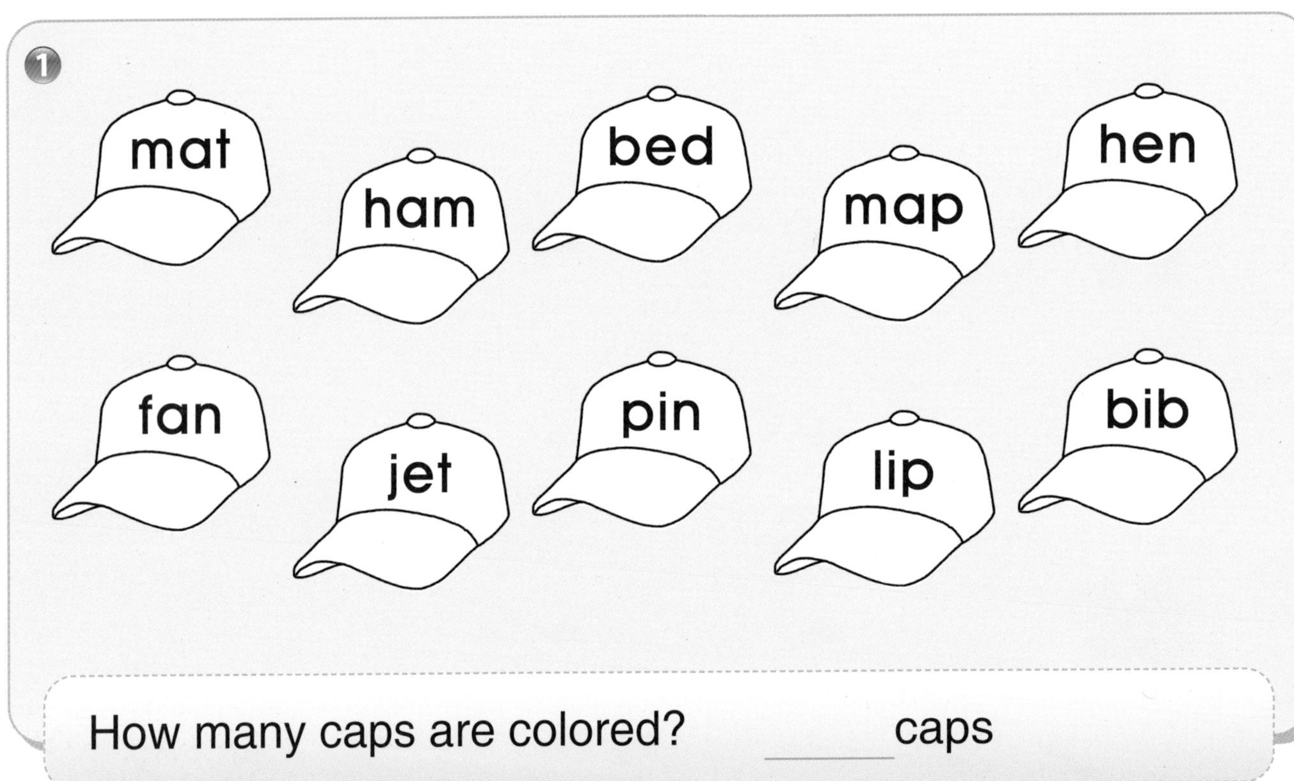

How many caps are colored? _______ caps

2

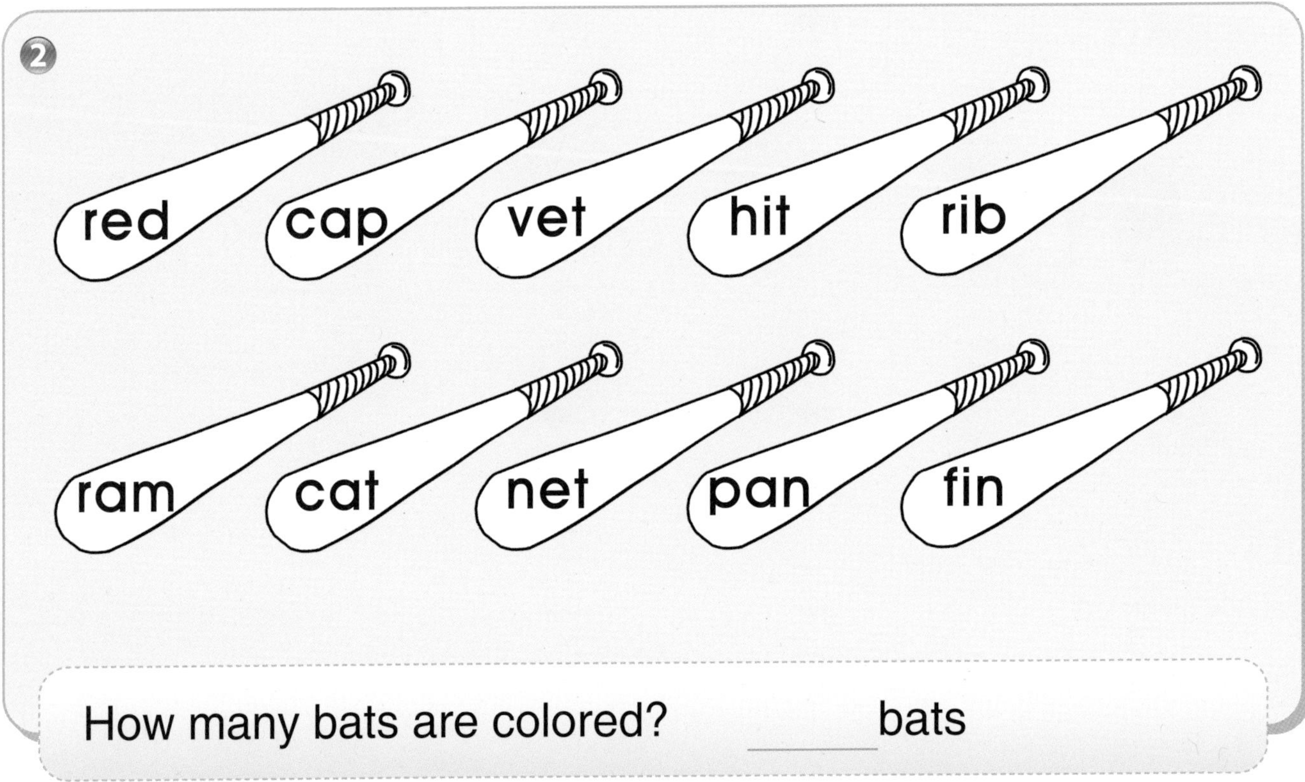

How many bats are colored? _______ bats

Listen and circle.

1. The cat sits on the  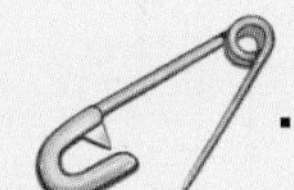 .

2. The pig has a 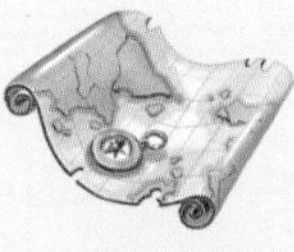  .

3. 6 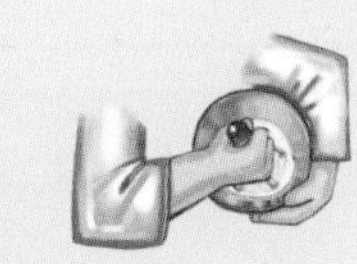 ribs are in the pan.

4. The   is on the dam.

5. The jam is in the 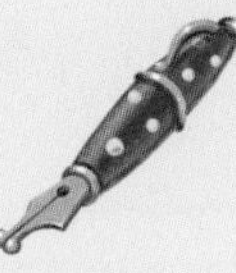  .

6. The man has a 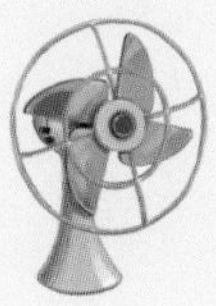  .

7. The red   sits on the mat.

Track 23

Read along!

Story by e-future
Pictures by Jeong Gyeom Kim

Story

Sight Words	a	and	are	goes	has	in	over	sees	the	with

Song

Track 24 Sing along!

What will they do?

The kid with the bat
has a six on his cap.
What will he do?

The vet with the bib
has the cat on her lap.
What will she do?

The man with the hat
has the ham in the pan.
What will he do?

The hen with the fan
has a wig for a bed.
What will she do?

Sight Words a do for has he her his in she the they what will with

Do the puzzle and find out.

h	1 ___	m
2 ___	i	p
j	3 ___	t
b	e	4 ___
5 ___	i	t
m	6 ___	n
b	a	7 ___

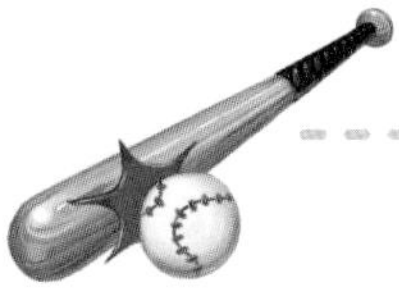

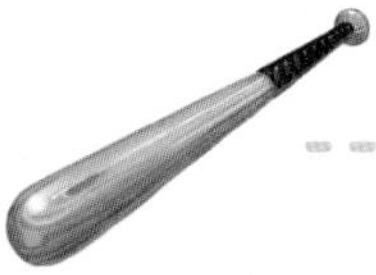

What does it say?

1 ___ 2 ___ 3 ___ 4 ___ 5 ___ 6 ___ 7 ___

Choose, write and match.

nap sit map

The kid has a ______________.

The man has a ______________.

The cats ______________ on the bed.

Cats' Cards

What you need: Book 2 flashcards (1~40), a die and counters

How to play:

1. Divide the flashcards evenly among teams.
2. Place the counters on "Start."
3. Take turns rolling the die and moving the counters.
4. Sound out the letters on the square. Find a flashcard with the matching letters, say the word, and discard the card on the board.
5. If the counter lands on "Switch," switch the counters among teams. If the counter lands on "Take," take a card from the pile and say the word. If the counter lands on "Drop," discard any card and say the word.
6. The team which first discards all the cards wins the game.

Cats' Cards
Start
am
ap
ed
ib
id
Drop
1
an
at
en
ig
in
am
ap
et
ip
it
Drop
1
an
at
Switch!
et
ix
ip
am
ap
ed
id
ib
Take
1
an
at
en
ig
in
am
ap
et
ip
it
at
ix
Finish
How to play
WHAT YOU NEED:
Book 2 flashcards (1~40), a die and counters
HOW TO PLAY: 1. Divide the flashcards evenly among teams.
2. Place the counters on "Start."
3. Take turns rolling the die and moving the counters.
4. Sound out the letters on the square. Find a flashcard with the matching letters, say the word, and discard the card on the board.
5. If the counter lands on "Switch," switch the counters among teams. If the counter lands on "Take," take a card from the pile and say the word. If the counter lands on "Drop," discard any card and say the word.
6. The team which first discards all the cards wins the game.

UNIT 6 Short Vowel O

Track 25

Listen and repeat.

Step 1

Step 2

o t → h o t

o t → p o t

o x → b o x

o x → f o x

Listen and repeat.

Step 1

Step 2

o p → c o p

o p → h o p

o g → d o g

o g → l o g

Look, choose and write.

1

2

3

4

5
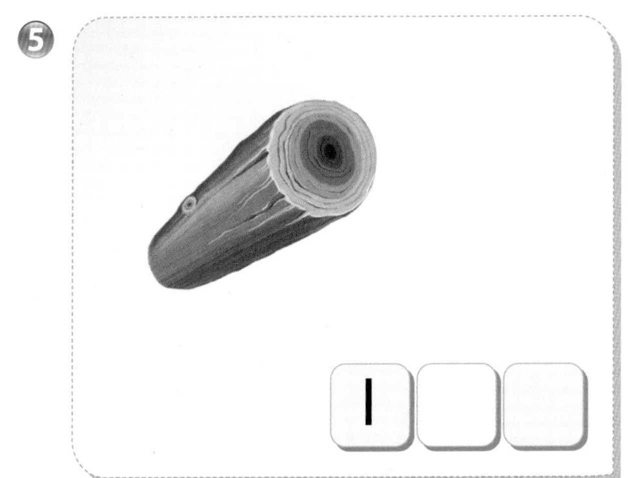

6

 Find and circle.

b	m	d	h	o	p
c	o	p	o	k	n
b	d	e	t	i	l
l	o	t	a	j	o
r	p	x	d	o	g

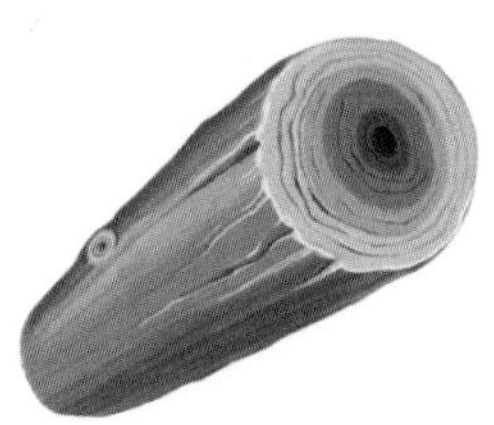

Track 27

Listen, match and circle.

1

d		o t
h		o g

2

c		o t
p		o p

3

d		o g
h		o t

4

b		o x
h		o p

5

f		o g
l		o x

6

d		o x
b		o g

Look, circle and write.

1. dog fox log

   The __________ is in the box.

2. hop pot cop

   The __________ is on the box.

3. cop log pot

   A dog is on the __________.

4. box hot cop

   The fox is __________.

5. pot fox log

   The dog has a hot __________.

Story

Track 28

Read along!

The fox hops on the box.
She is hot.

The dog hops on the log.
She is hot.

The fox sits on the mat.
The dog sits on the mat.
They are not hot.

Sight Words	are	is	not	on	she	the	they

Trace and write.

1  o → og → dog dog

2 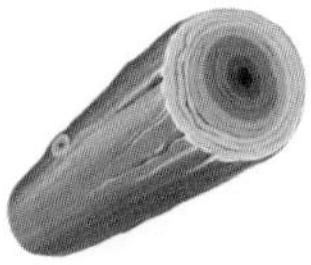 o → →

3  o → op → cop cop

4  o → →

5  o → ot → hot hot

6  o → →

7  o → ox → box box

8  o → →

UNIT 7 Short Vowel U

Track 29

Listen and repeat.

Step 1

Step 2

u g → b u g

u g → h u g

u g → m u g

u g → r u g

Listen and repeat.

Step 1

Step 2

u b → r u b

u b → t u b

u p → c u p

u p → p u p

Look, choose and write.

u g

u p

① 

b

② 

t

③ 

m

④ 

p

⑤ 

r

⑥ 

h

Find and circle.

r	c	d	g	o	p
t	u	b	o	k	m
b	p	u	p	r	u
l	o	t	r	u	g
b	u	g	r	b	b

Track 31

Listen, match and circle.

1

b ·	· u b
t ·	· u g

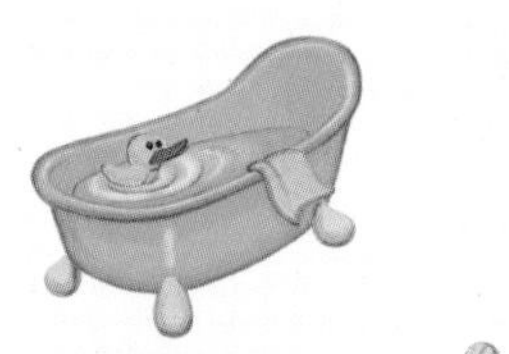

2

m ·	· u g
p ·	· u p

3

h ·	· u b
r ·	· u g

4

c ·	· u p
r ·	· u g

5

b ·	· u p
p ·	· u g

6

r ·	· u g
t ·	· u b

 Look, circle and write.

1

bug pup cup

The __________ has a mug.

2

mug bug hug

The __________ is on the cup.

3

rug bug rub

The pup is under the __________.

4

hop tub hug

The two bugs __________.

5

rub mug tub

The pup is in the __________.

Story

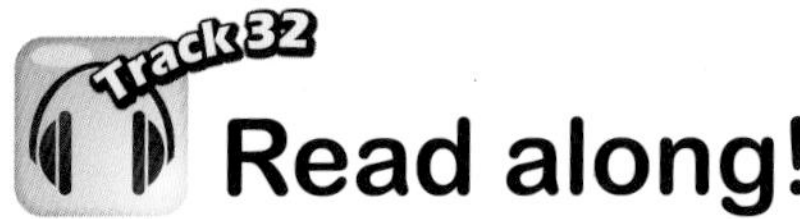

Track 32 Read along!

Six bugs sit on the mug.

One bug hops on the mug.

Six bugs hop on the mug.

One bug is in the mug.

Six bugs are in the mug.

They hop and hug in the mug.

Sight Words: and are in is on one the they

Trace and write.

1. u → ug → bug bug
2. u → →
3. u → →
4. u → →
5. u → ub → rub rub
6. u → →
7. u → up → cup cup
8. u → →

UNIT 8 Short Vowel U

Listen and repeat.

Step 1

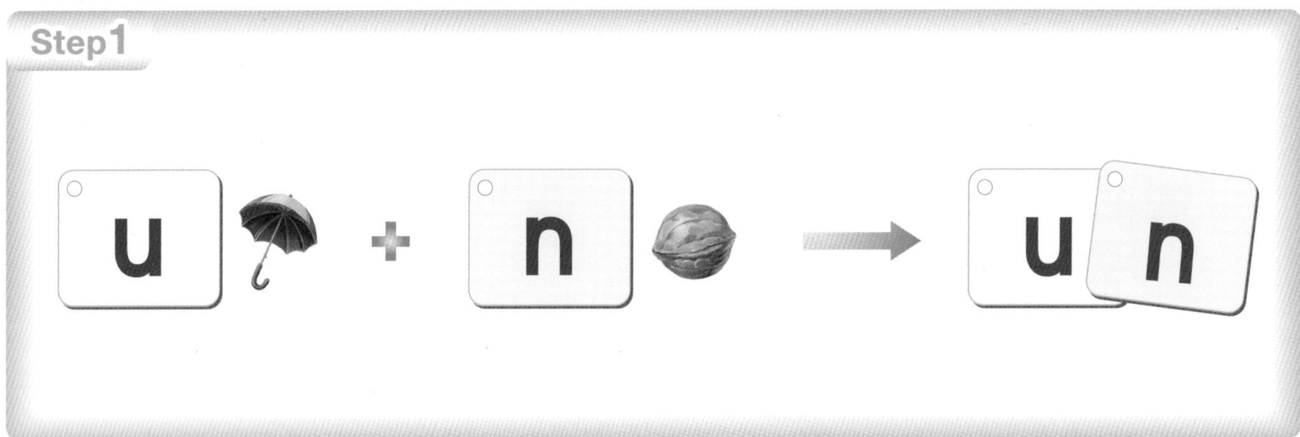

Step 2

un → bun

un → gun

un → run

un → sun

Listen and repeat.

Step 1

Step 2

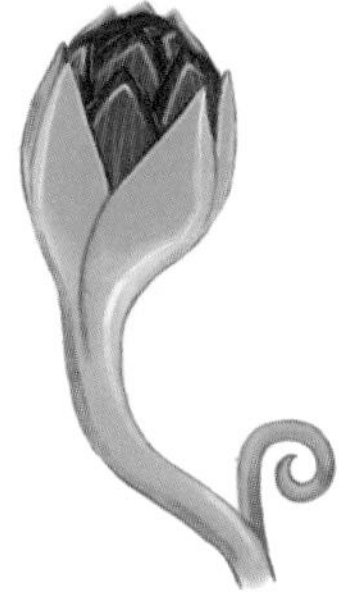

u d → b u d

u d → m u d

u t → c u t

u t → n u t

Look, choose and write.

u n

u t

1 

2 

3 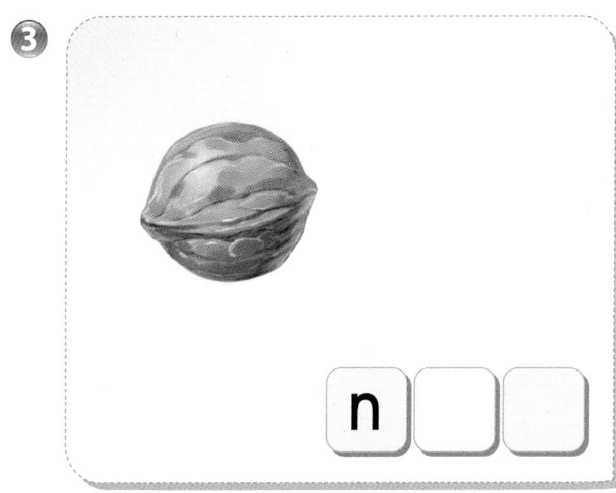

4 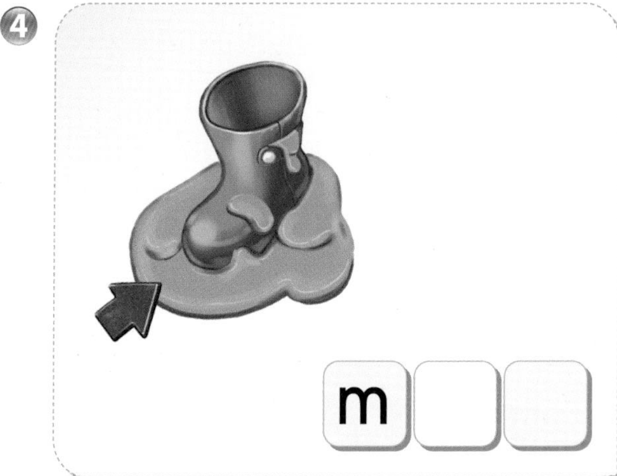

5 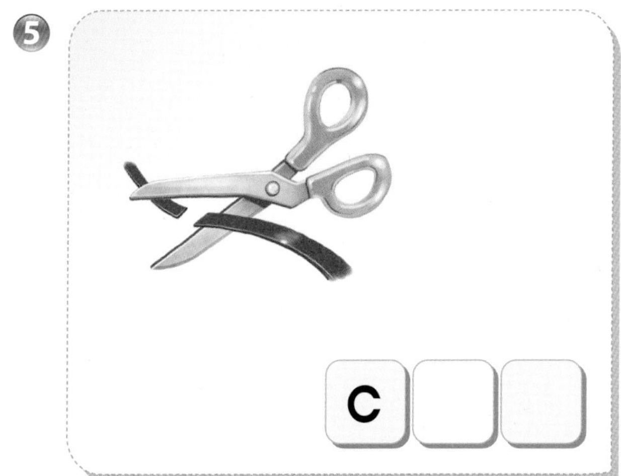

6 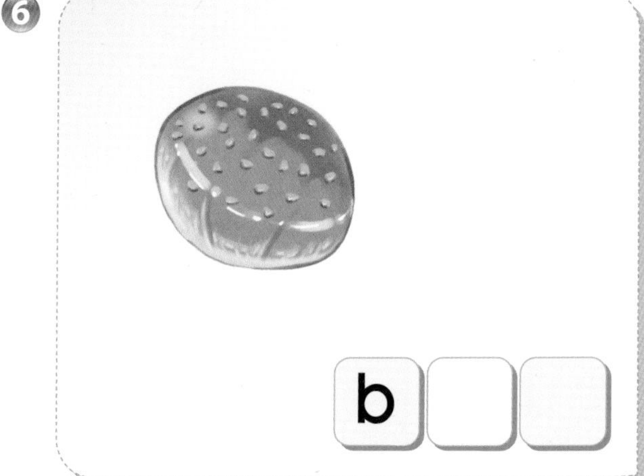

 **Find and circle.**

r	c	u	t	r	p
n	s	b	z	u	b
u	p	u	x	n	u
t	b	u	n	s	d
b	w	m	g	u	n

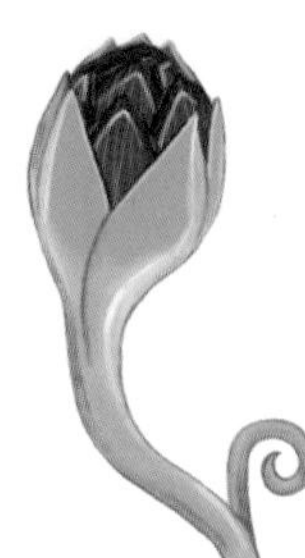

Listen, match and circle.

1.
- b · · u d
- m · · u n

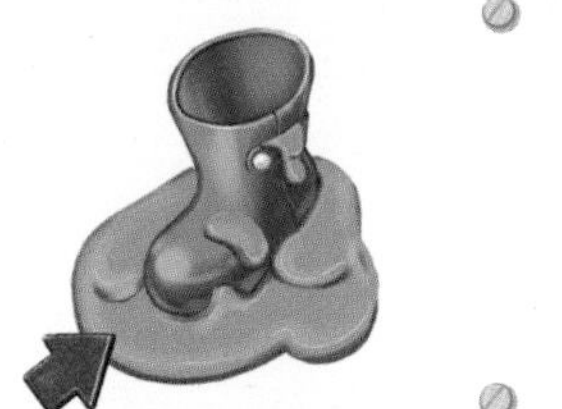

2.
- c · · u t
- g · · u n

3.
- b · · u n
- r · · u d

4.
- n · · u n
- s · · u t

5.
- b · · u n
- c · · u t

6.
- m · · u n
- s · · u d

 Look, circle and write.

1

run sun bun

The __________ is in the sky.

2

run gun sun

The pups __________ to the ham.

3

nut bun gun

The __________ is in the pan.

4

gun bud cut

The kids __________ the mat.

5

mud run bun

The gun is in the __________.

Story

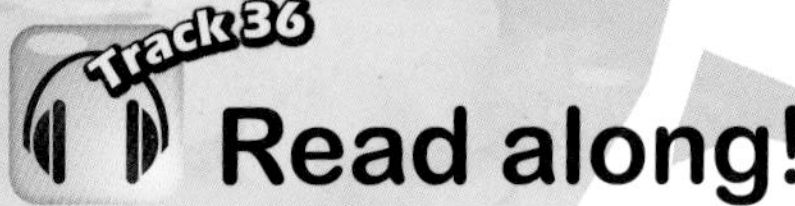

Track 36 Read along!

The pup cuts the nut.
The bug is in the nut.

The bug runs.
The bug is in the mud.

The bug runs.
The bug is in the sun.

"Sorry, bug!" says the pup.

Sight Words in is says sorry the

Trace and write.

1. u → un → bun bun
2. u → →
3. u → →
4. u → →
5. u → ud → bud bud
6. u → →
7. u → ut → cut cut
8. u → →

REVIEW 2 Short Vowels O · U

Track 37

Listen and color.

1

How many cups are colored? ______ cups

2

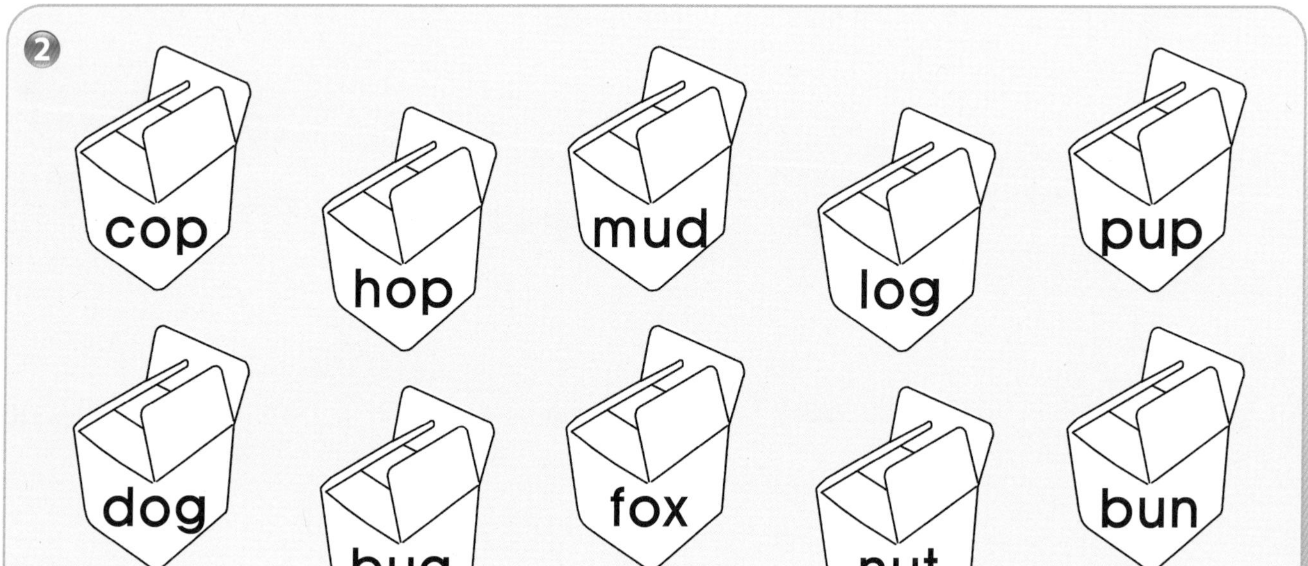

How many boxes are colored? ______ boxes

Listen and circle.

1. The 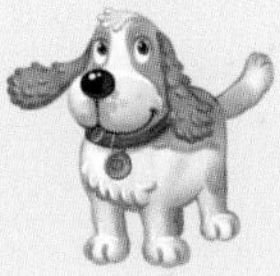 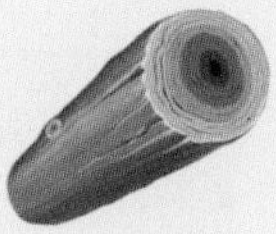 is in the box.

2. The fox is in the 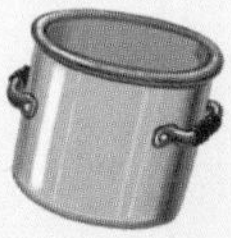 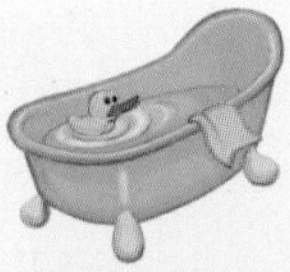 .

3. The 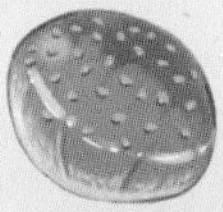 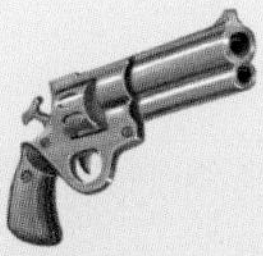 is in the hot pot.

4. The rug and the 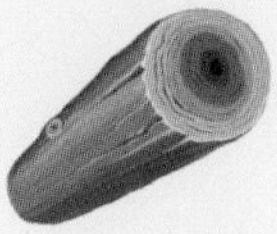 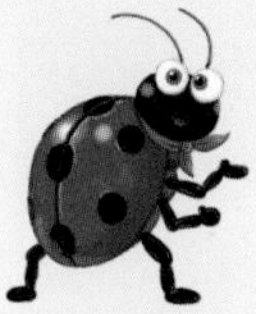 are wet.

5. The 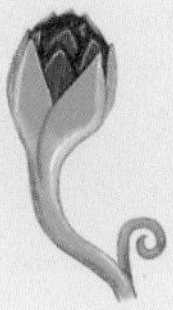 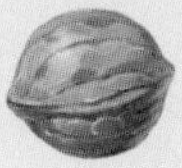 is in the mud.

6. The cop has a 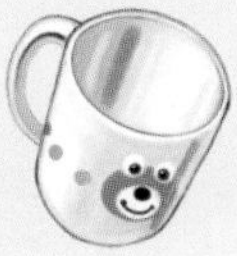 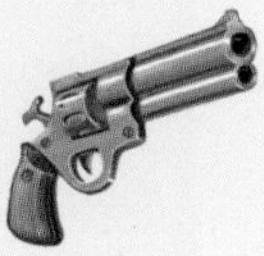 .

7. Mom and Dad 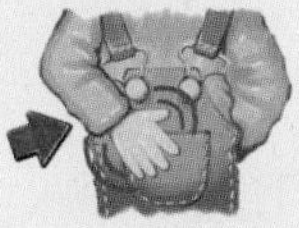 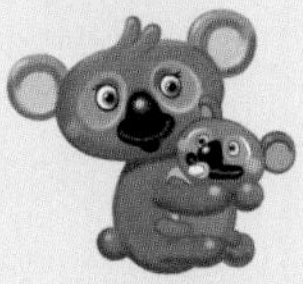 the kid.

Bob, Mub and the Cup

Read along!

Story by Jason Wilburn
Pictures by Jeong Gyeom Kim

Sight Words a and has in is it the to what

Song

Track 40

Sing along!

Where are they?

The bug with a mug
sits on the rug.

The pup with the bud
sits in the mud.

The fox with the nut
sits in the hut.

But, where is the dog?
He is in the log!

Sight Words a are but he in is on the they where with

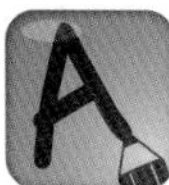

A Do the puzzle and find out.

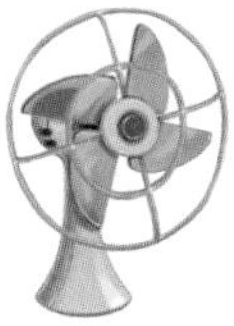

f 1 ___ n

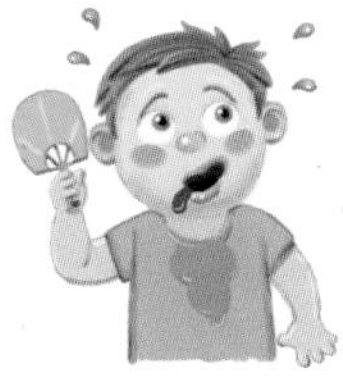

2 ___ o t

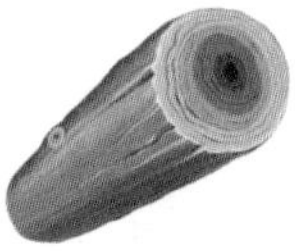

l 3 ___ g

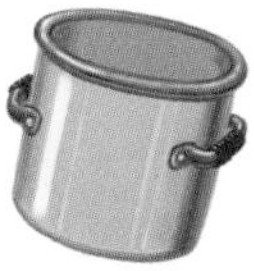

p o 4 ___

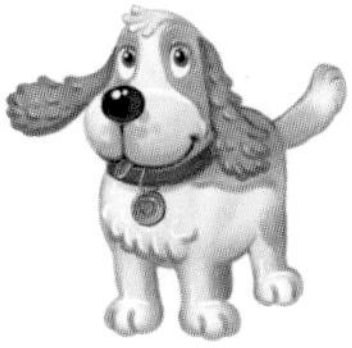

5 ___ o g

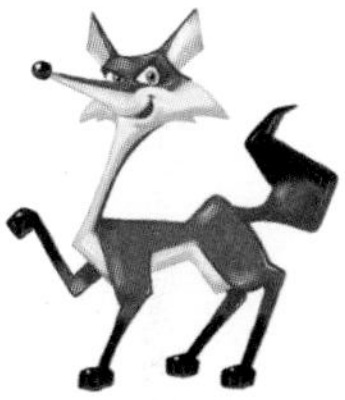

f 6 ___ x

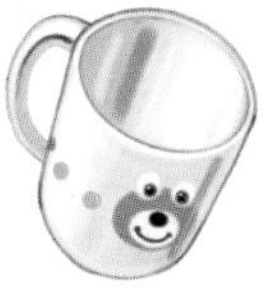

m u 7 ___

What does it say?

1 ___   2 ___ 3 ___ 4 ___   5 ___ 6 ___ 7 ___

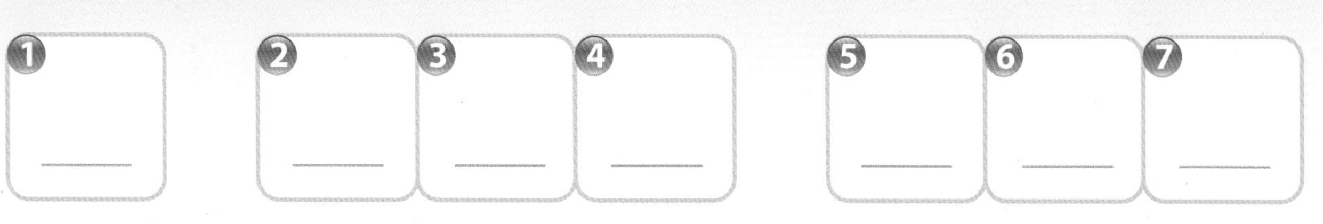

Choose, write and match.

bug hug tub

The kids ________ the ram.

The ________ is on the nut.

The pup is in the ________.

Treasure Hunt

What you need: a die and counters

How to play:

1. Place the counters on "Start."
2. Take turns rolling the die and moving the counters.
3. Read the word where the counter lands by combining the beginning letter in the vertical line and the ending letters in the horizontal line.
4. Get 1 to 4 points depending on the squares.
   1 point: monster
   2 points: no picture
   3 points: word picture
   4 points: treasure
5. The team which first arrives at "Finish" gets 2 extra points.
6. The team with the most points wins the game.

Treasure Hunt
ot
up
ut
op
ox
ud
ug
un
f
c
b
h
m
n
p
r
Start
Finish
1
2
3
4
5
6
7
8
9
10
11
12
13
14
15
16
17
18
19
20
21
22
23
24
25
26
27
28
29
30
31
32
33
34
35
36
37
38
39
40
41
42
43
44
45
46
47
48
49
50
51
52
WHAT YOU NEED: a die and counters
HOW TO PLAY:
1. Place the counters on "Start."
2. Take turns rolling the die and moving the counters.
3. Read the word where the counter lands by combining the beginning letter in the vertical line and the ending letters in the horizontal line.
4. Get 1 to 4 points depending on the squares.
1 point: monster
2 points: no picture
3 points: word picture
4 points: treasure
5. The team which first arrives at "Finish" gets 2 extra points, and the game ends.
6. The team with the most points wins the game.

CHALLENGE Short Vowels a·e·i·o·u

Listen and trace.

1

2
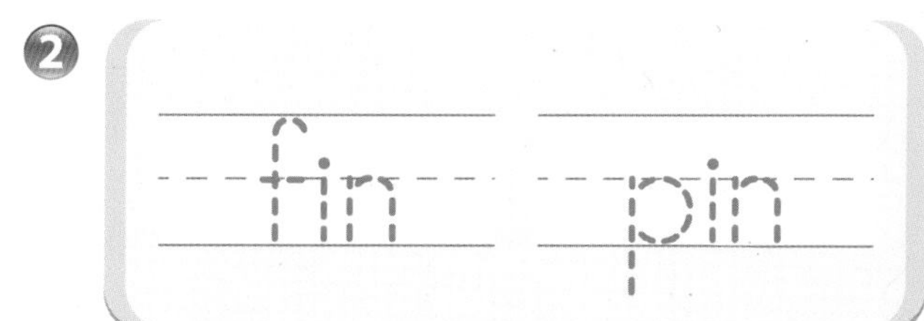

3
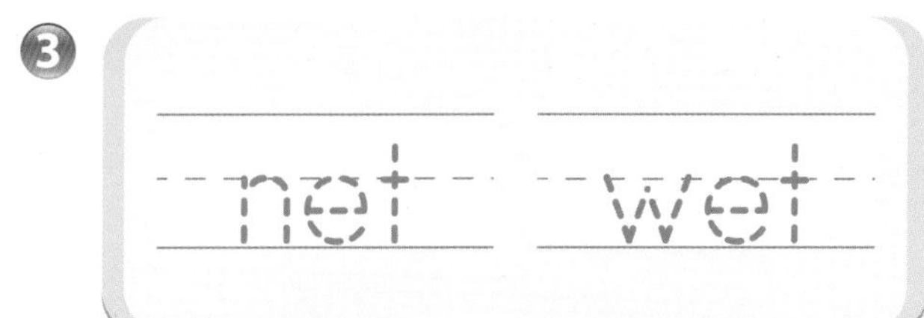

4
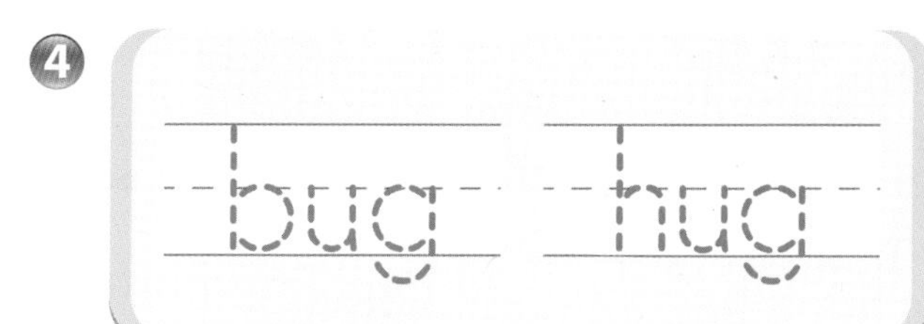

5
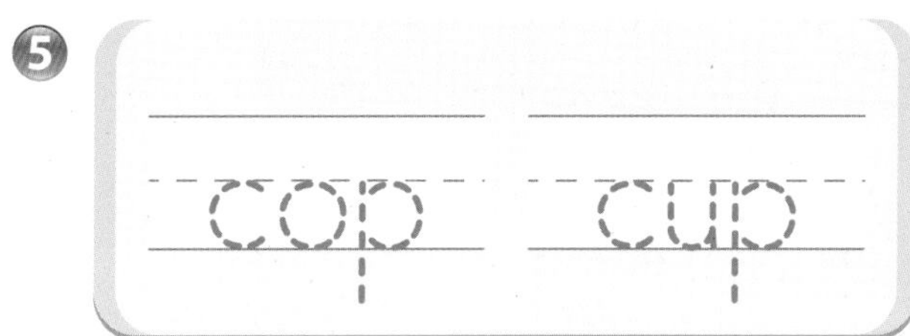

6
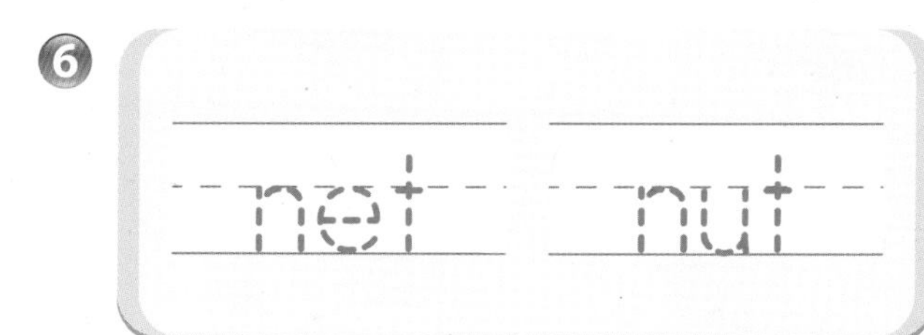

7
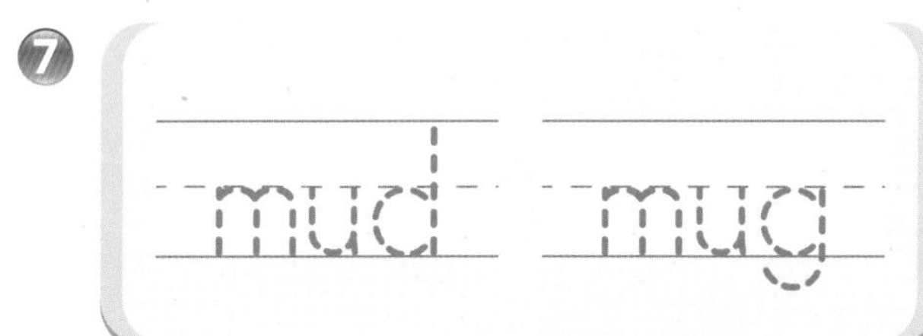

8

9
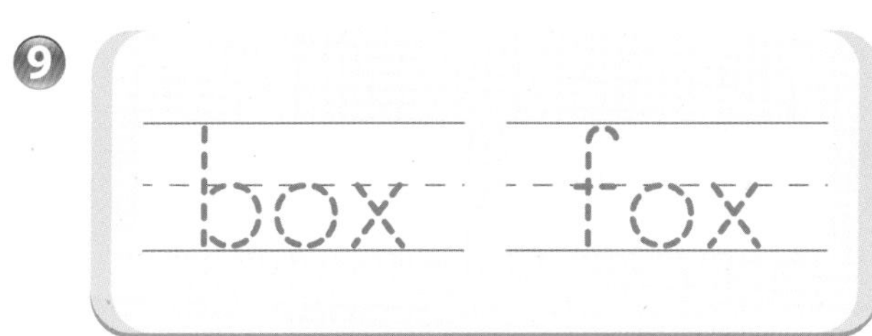

10
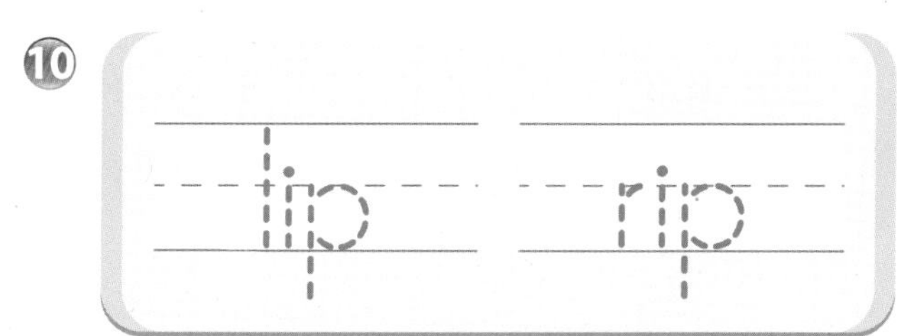

11

12
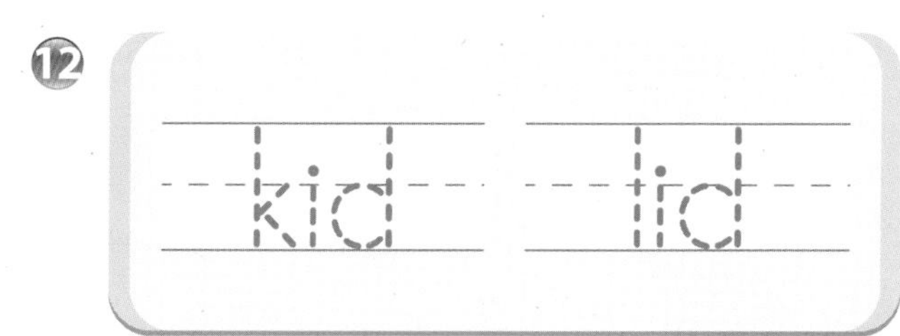

Listen and circle.

1. The kid has a 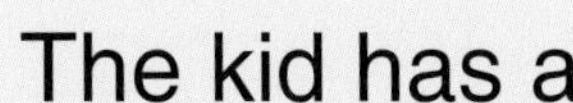   .

2. The   has a bib .

3. The ram has a 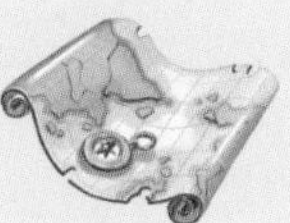  .

4. The   is on the mat.

5. The man has a  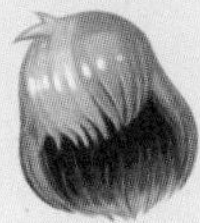 .

6. The bug is in the   .

7. The kid has a bun and   .

Ham for Pat

Track 43

Read along!

Story by Jason Wilburn
Pictures by Jeong Gyeom Kim

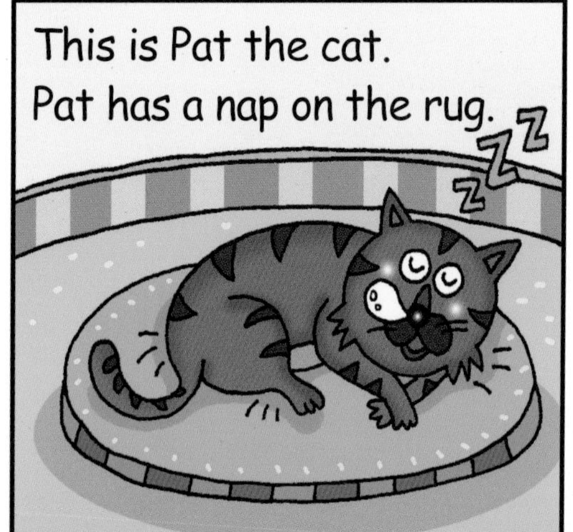

Sight Words a and for has have gives into is on sees sorry the they this to

Song
Track 44
Sing along!
The Cat's Jam
Pam and Jan have the ham in the pan.
They sit and mix the jam in the cup.
The cat hops up on Pam's lap.
Oh no! The cup is on Pam's lap.
Now, the cat is red.
cat
Sight Words
and have in is no now oh on the they

Look, circle and write.

1

dam | jam

dam

2
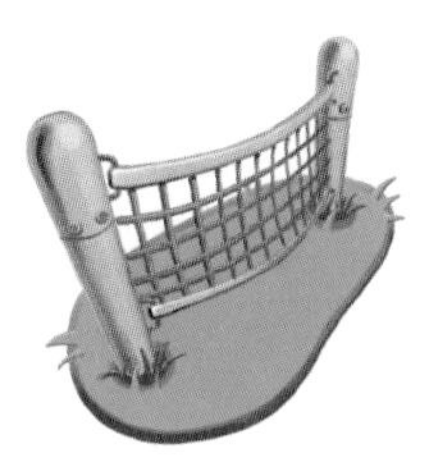

nut | net

3

bun | gun

4

net | wet

5

fan | pan

6

box | fox

7

fin | pin

8

hot | hop

9

rib | bib

A Look, choose and write.

fan hot sun

① The dog sits in the ____________.

② The dog is ____________.

③ The dog has a ____________.

cop rib pan

① The ____________ has a bib.

② The rib is in the ____________.

③ The ____________ is hot.

Short Vowel Race

What you need: Book 2 flashcards (1~64), a pouch and counters

How to play:

1. Place the counters on "Start."
2. Put the flashcards in the pouch.
3. Take turns drawing a flashcard from the pouch.
4. Say the word and move the counter to the nearest matching vowel.
5. The team which first arrives at "Finish" wins the game.

Short Vowel Race
START
FINISH
Go Back 3 Spaces
Go Back 4 Spaces
Go Back 5 Spaces
ABCDEF
apple
banana
WHAT YOU NEED: Book 2 flashcards (1~64), a pouch and counters
HOW TO PLAY:
1. Place the counters on "Start."
2. Put the flashcards in the pouch.
3. Take turns drawing a flashcard from the pouch.
4. Say the word and move the counter to the nearest matching vowel.
5. The team which first arrives at "Finish" wins the game.

PROGRESS TEST

Name		Date		Total Score	/ 100

PART 1

Score:

	Points	Correct	Incorrect
1	3		
2	3		
3	3		
4	3		
5	3		
6	3		
7	3		
8	3		
9	3		
10	3		
11	3		
12	3		
13	3		
14	3		
15	3		

PART 2

Score:

	Points	Correct	Incorrect
16	3		
17	3		
18	3		
19	3		
20	3		
21	4		
22	4		
23	4		
24	4		
25	4		
26	4		
27	4		
28	4		
29	4		
30	4		

Recommendation		
	0~50 points	Need to study Book 2 again
	51~75 points	Need to review Book 2
	76~100 points	Ready to move on to Book 3

Part 1

Track 45 Listen and check. 1 ~ 3

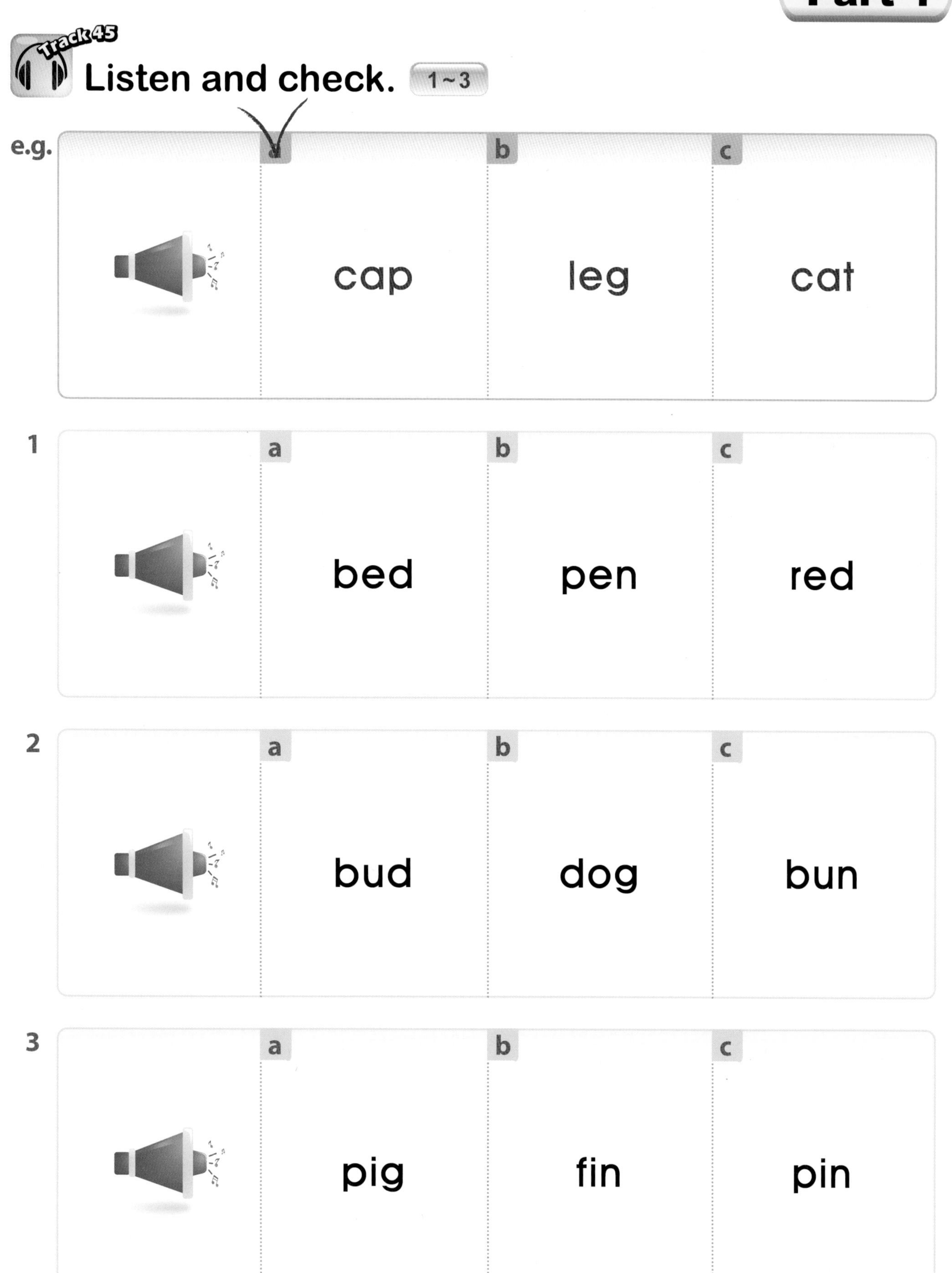

Track 46

Look, listen and check. 4~6

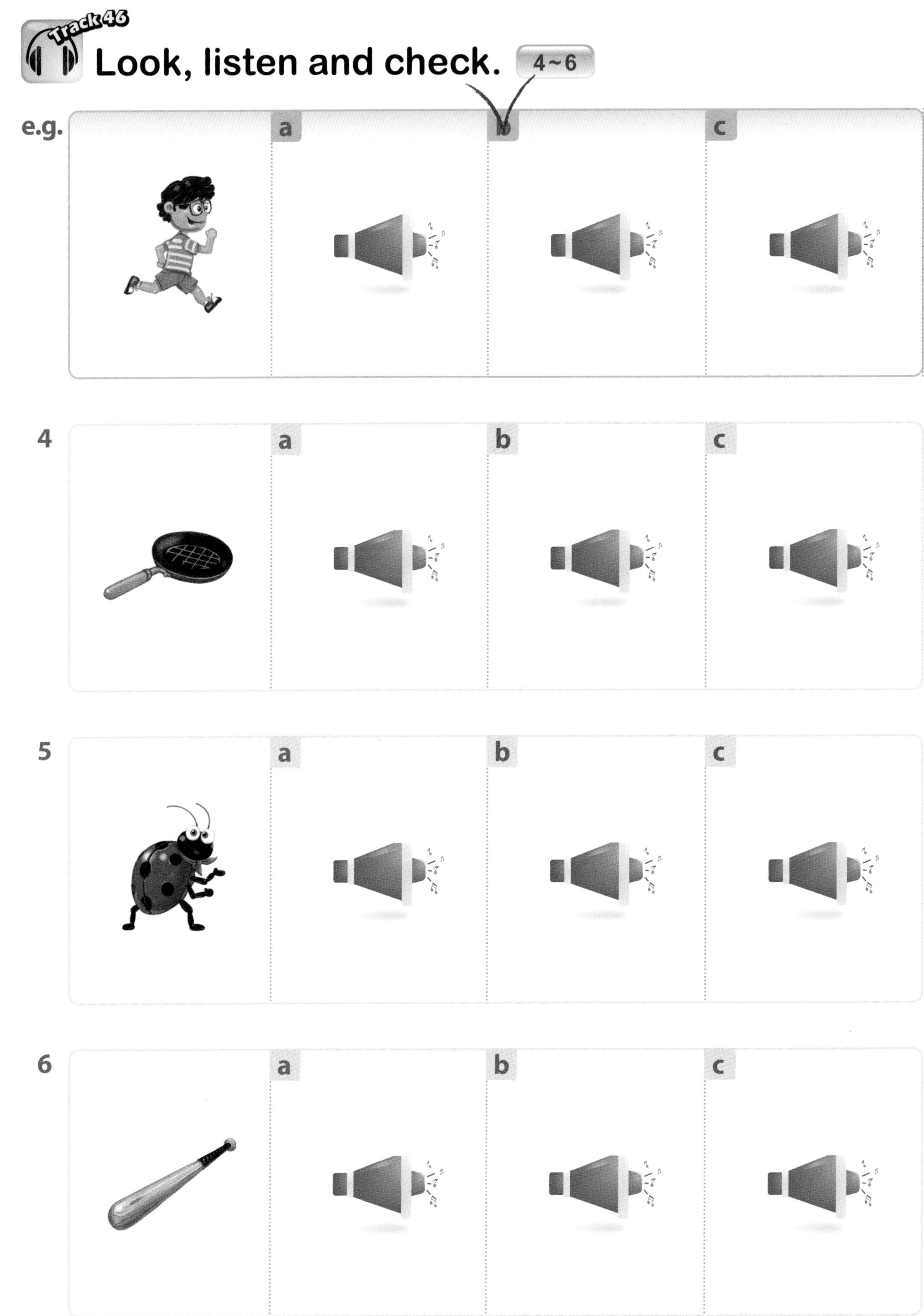

Track 47

Listen and check. 7~9

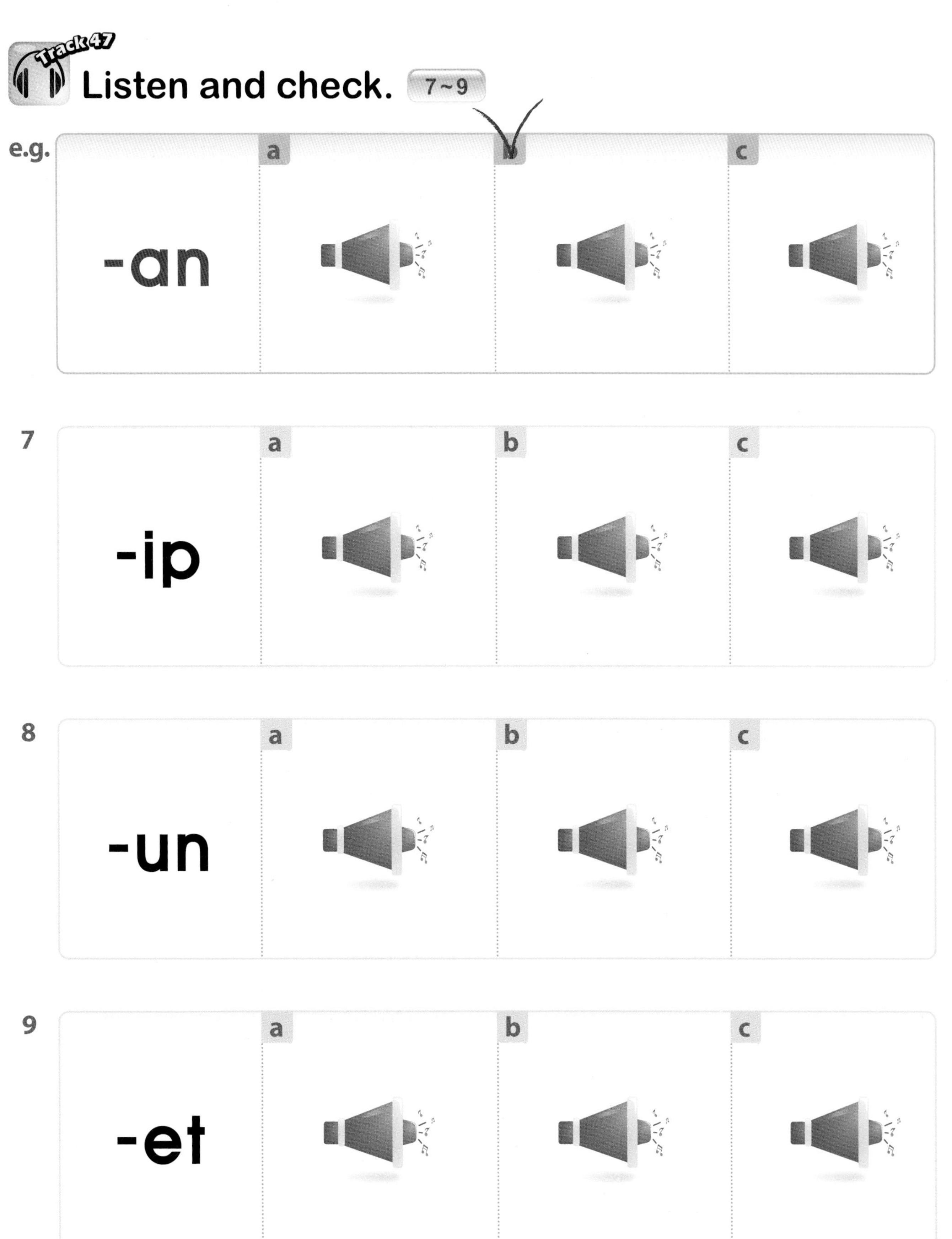

Track 48 Listen and write. 10~12

e.g.

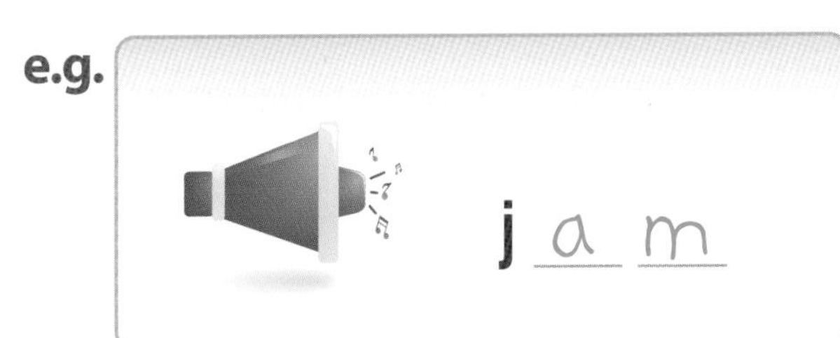

10

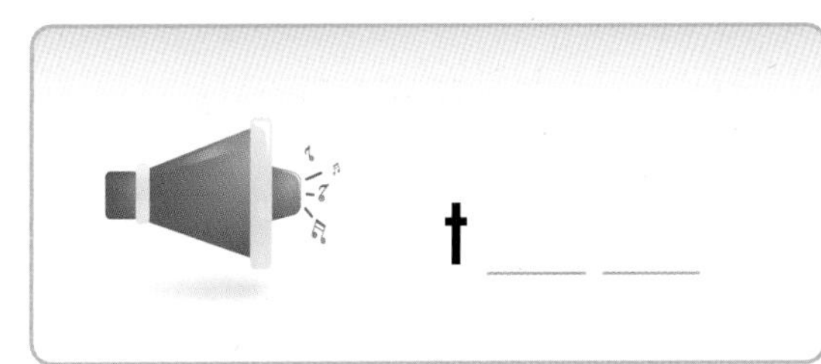

11

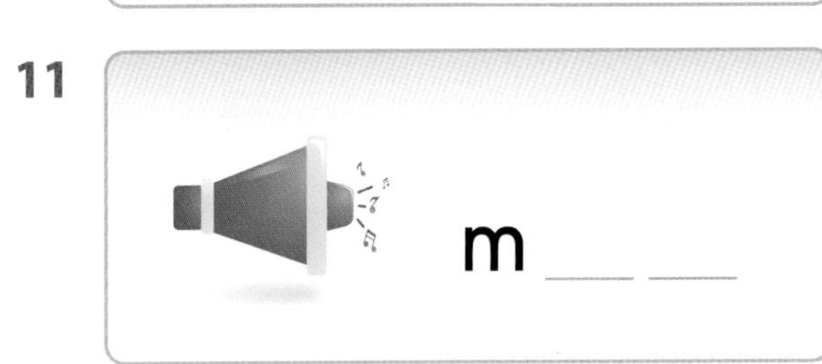

12

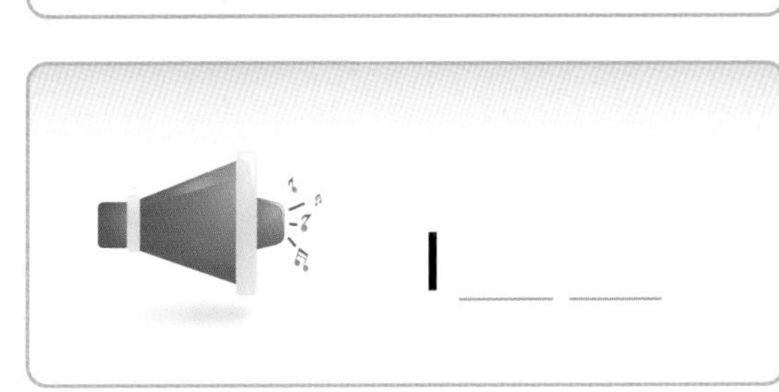

Track 49 Listen and check. 13~15

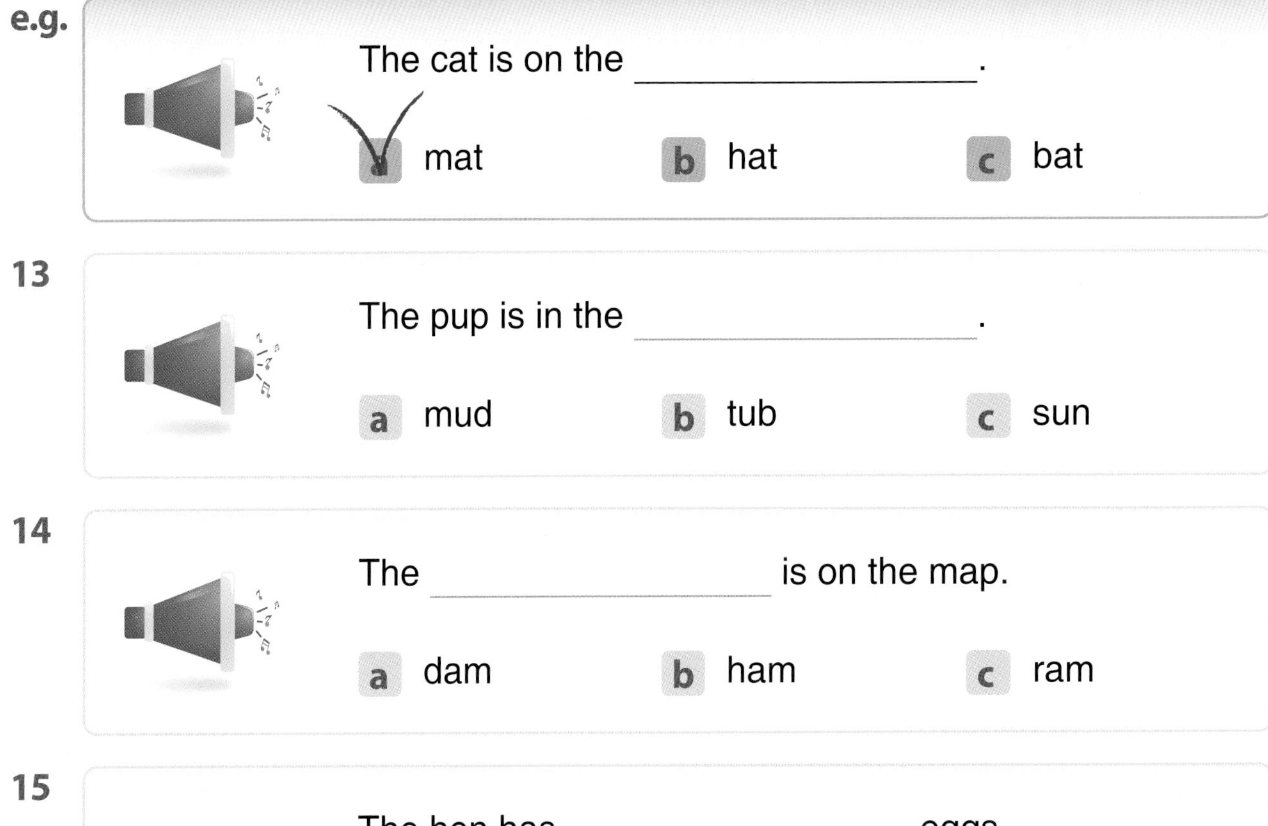

e.g. The cat is on the ____________.

a mat b hat c bat

13 The pup is in the ____________.

a mud b tub c sun

14 The ____________ is on the map.

a dam b ham c ram

15 The hen has ____________ eggs.

a wet b red c six

Look and check. 16~18

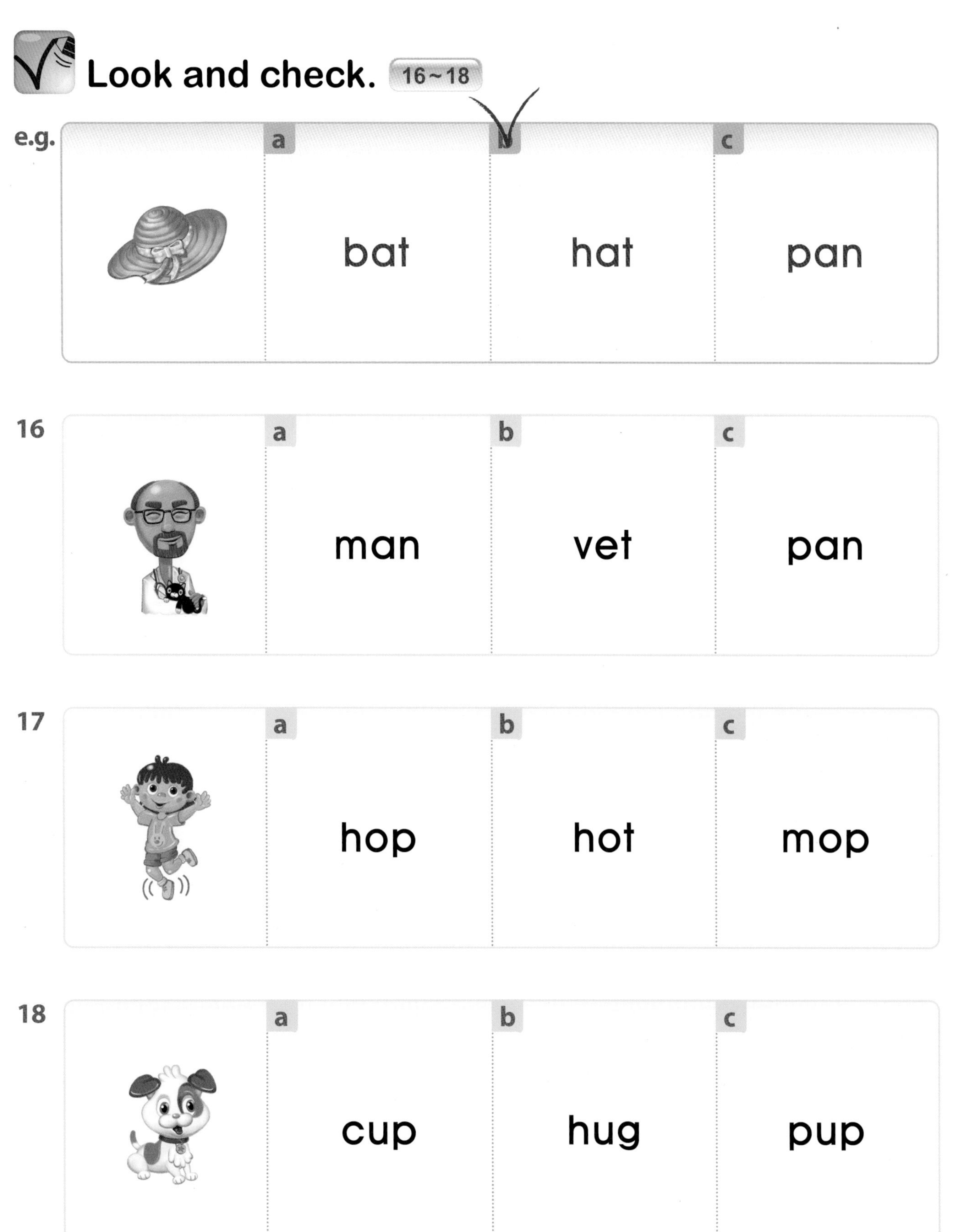

	a	b	c
e.g.	bat	hat	pan
16	man	vet	pan
17	hop	hot	mop
18	cup	hug	pup

Circle the pictures that rhyme. 19~21

e.g.

19

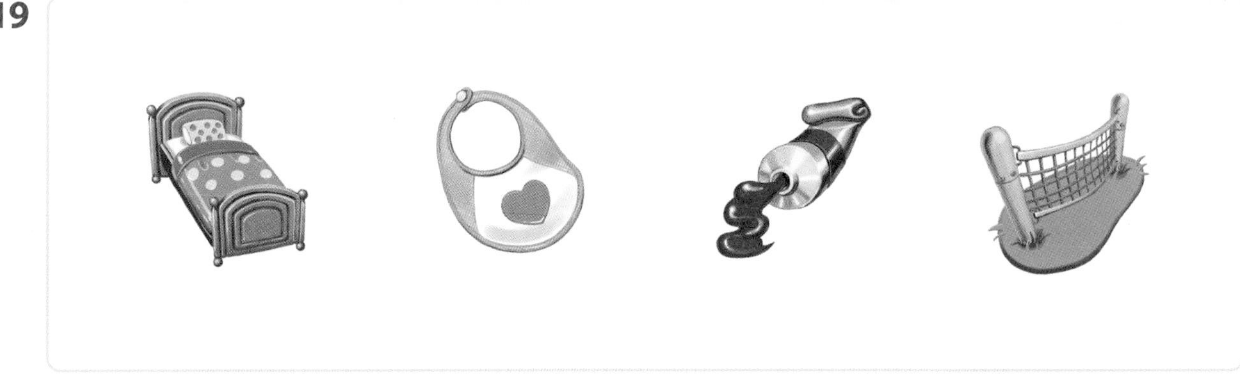

20

21

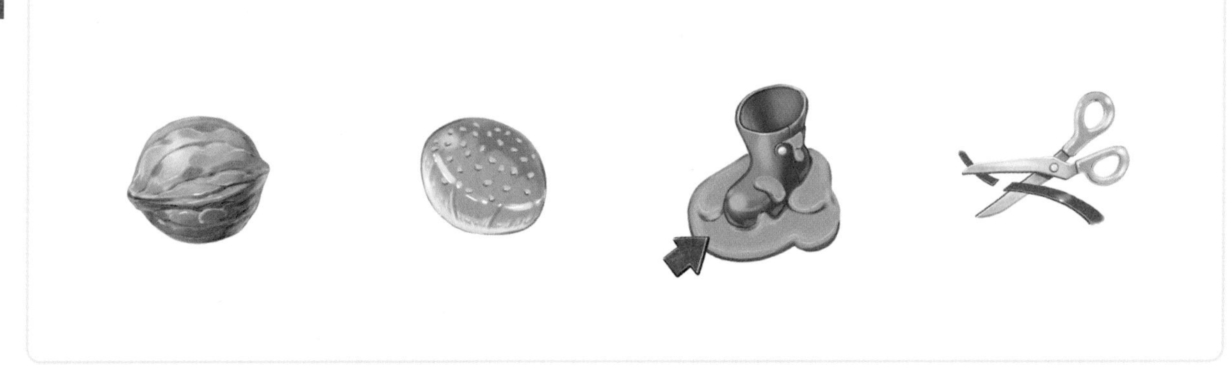

Look and write. 22~27

e.g.

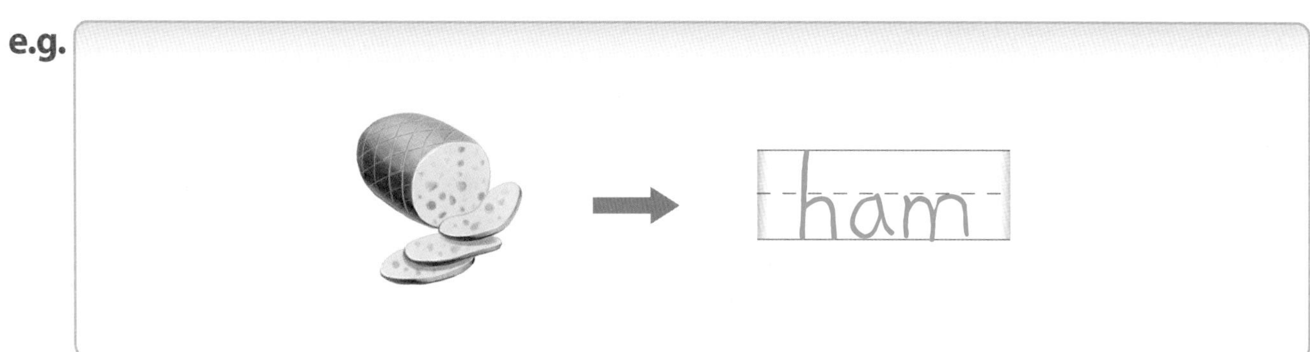

22

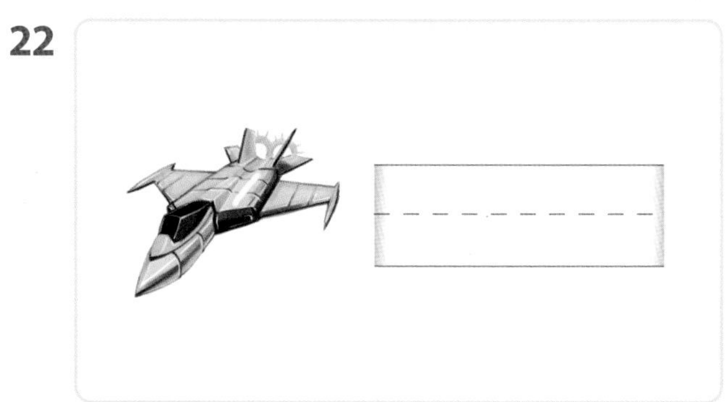

23

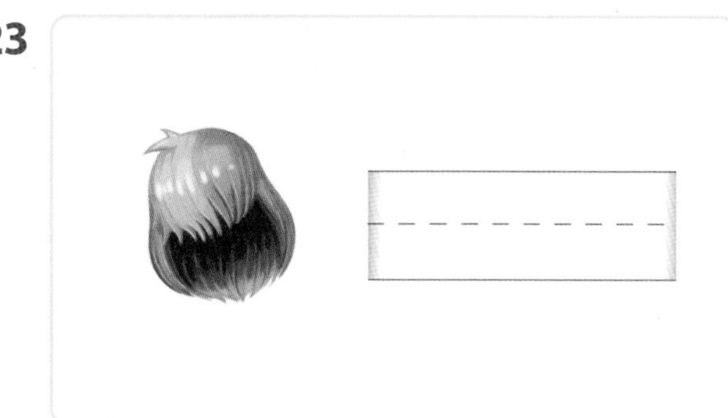

24

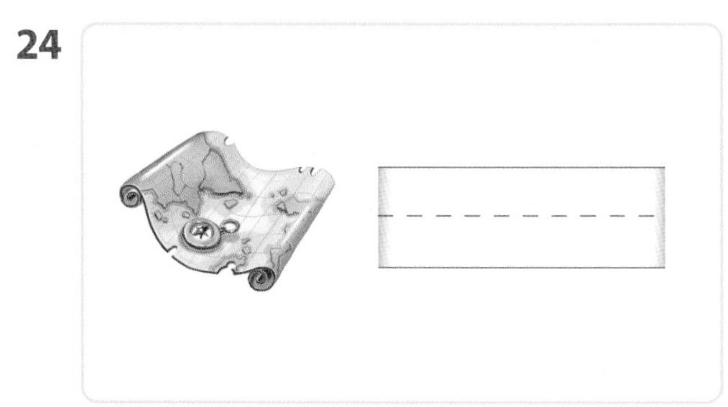

25

26

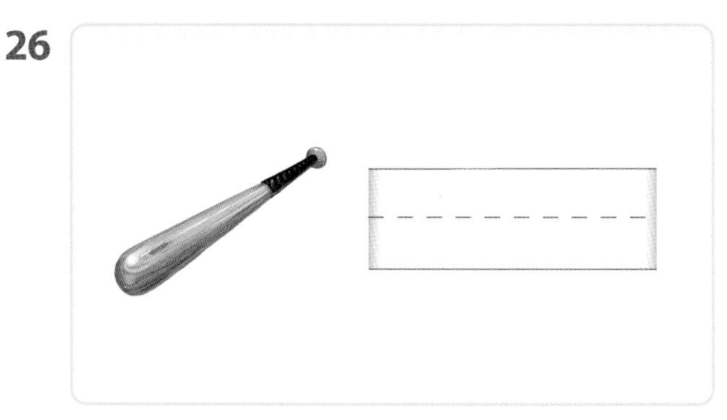

27

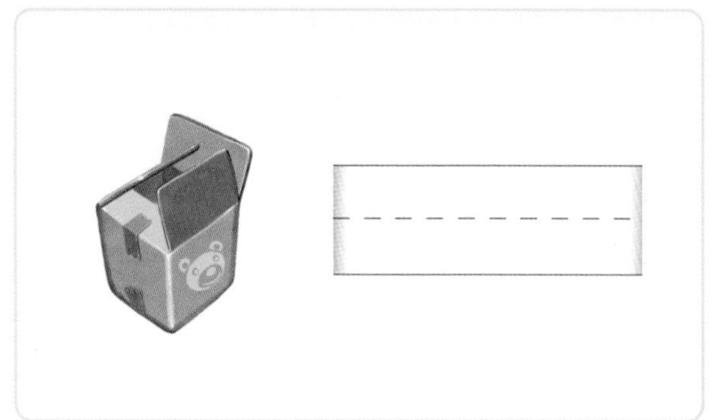

Look, read and write. 28 ~ 30

e.g.

The cop is on the ___box___.

28

A rip is on the ______________.

29

The kid has a ______________.

30

The kids cut the ______________.

Smart Phonics 2

Sight Words
in Songs, Stories and Comics

Flashcards 2

1. dam
2. ham
3. jam
4. ram
5. cap
6. lap
7. map
8. nap
9. can
10. fan
11. man
12. pan
13. bat
14. cat
15. hat
16. mat
17. jet
18. net
19. vet
20. wet
21. bed
22. red
23. hen
24. pen
25. bib
26. rib
27. kid
28. lid
29. pig
30. wig
31. fin
32. pin
33. dip
34. hip
35. lip
36. rip
37. hit
38. sit
39. mix
40. six
41. dog
42. log
43. cop
44. hop
45. hot
46. pot
47. box
48. fox
49. bug
50. hug
51. mug
52. rug
53. rub
54. tub
55. cup
56. pup
57. bun
58. gun
59. run
60. sun
61. bud
62. mud
63. cut
64. nut

Smart Phonics

Flashcards

Use these flashcards for playing games.

B2 01	B2 02	B2 03	B2 04
B2 05	B2 06	B2 07	B2 08
B2 09	B2 10	B2 11	B2 12
B2 13	B2 14	B2 15	B2 16

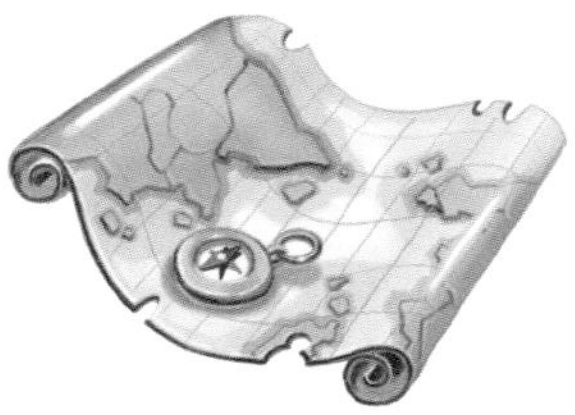

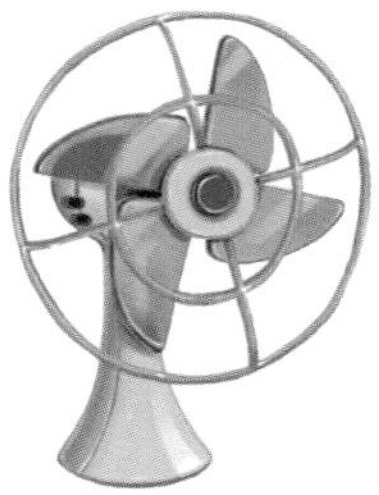

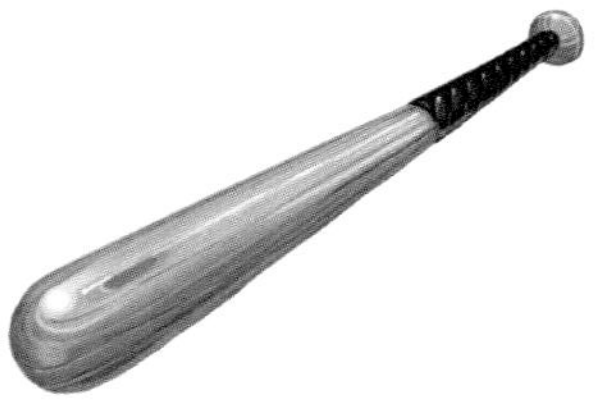

B2 4 ram	B2 3 jam	B2 2 ham	B2 1 dam
B2 8 nap	B2 7 map	B2 6 lap	B2 5 cap
B2 12 pan	B2 11 man	B2 10 fan	B2 9 can
B2 16 mat	B2 15 hat	B2 14 cat	B2 13 bat

Flashcards

Use these flashcards for playing games.

B2 17	B2 18	B2 19	B2 20
B2 21	B2 22	B2 23	B2 24
B2 25	B2 26	B2 27	B2 28
B2 29	B2 30	B2 31	B2 32

B2 20 wet	B2 19 vet	B2 18 net	B2 17 jet
B2 24 pen	B2 23 hen	B2 22 red	B2 21 bed
B2 28 lid	B2 27 kid	B2 26 rib	B2 25 bib
B2 32 pin	B2 31 fin	B2 30 wig	B2 29 pig

Flashcards

Use these flashcards for playing games.

B2 33	B2 34	B2 35	B2 36
B2 37	B2 38	B2 39	B2 40
B2 41	B2 42	B2 43	B2 44
B2 45	B2 46	B2 47	B2 48

B2 36 rip	B2 35 lip	B2 34 hip	B2 33 dip
B2 40 six	B2 39 mix	B2 38 sit	B2 37 hit
B2 44 hop	B2 43 cop	B2 42 log	B2 41 dog
B2 48 fox	B2 47 box	B2 46 pot	B2 45 hot

Flashcards

Use these flashcards for playing games.

B2 49	B2 50	B2 51	B2 52
B2 53	B2 54	B2 55	B2 56
B2 57	B2 58	B2 59	B2 60
B2 61	B2 62	B2 63	B2 64

B2 52	B2 51	B2 50	B2 49
rug	**mug**	**hug**	**bug**
B2 56	B2 55	B2 54	B2 53
pup	**cup**	**tub**	**rub**
B2 60	B2 59	B2 58	B2 57
sun	**run**	**gun**	**bun**
B2 64	B2 63	B2 62	B2 61
nut	**cut**	**mud**	**bud**